BUSINESS WORDS
YOU SHOULD
KNOW

From Accelerated Depreciation to Zero-based Budgeting—Learn the Lingo for Any Field

H. DEAN McKAY, Ph.D., AND P.T. SHANK

Adamsmedia

Avon, Massachusetts

I dedicate this book to Susan Shank Mix, my wife, lifelong friend, and trusted advisor. Without her encouragement, creativity, and support, this book would be still in my imagination. —Dr. Dean McKay

I dedicate this book to Al Burgos, an accountant with the heart of an astronomer, because without him, no deadline would have been made. —P. T. Shank

Published by
Adams Media, an F+W Publications Company
57 Littlefield Street, Avon, MA 02322. U.S.A.
www.adamsmedia.com

ISBN 10: 1-59869-146-5
ISBN 13: 978-1-59869-146-7

Printed in Canada.
J I H G F E D C B A

Library of Congress Cataloging-in-Publication Data
McKay, H. Dean.
Business words you should know /
H. Dean McKay, and P.T. Shank.
p. cm.
ISBN-13: 978-1-59869-146-7 (pbk.)
ISBN-10: 1-59869-146-5 (pbk.)
1. Business—Dictionaries. I. Shank, P. T. II. Title.
HF1001.M26 2007
650.03—dc22   2007016518

This publication is designed to provide accurate and authoritative information with regard to the subject matter covered. It is sold with the understanding that the publisher is not engaged in rendering legal, accounting, or other professional advice. If legal advice or other expert assistance is required, the services of a competent professional person should be sought.
—From a *Declaration of Principles* jointly adopted by a Committee of the American Bar Association and a Committee of Publishers and Associations

Many of the designations used by manufacturers and sellers to distinguish their product are claimed as trademarks. Where those designations appear in this book and Adams Media was aware of a trademark claim, the designations have been printed with initial capital letters.

This book is available at quantity discounts for bulk purchases.
For information, please call 1–800–289–0963.

Contents

Acknowledgments

This book is an accumulation of decades of business, education, and management with some remarkable mentors and associates. In particular, I would like to recognize my mentors at the Peter F. Drucker Center for Management, Claremont Graduate School, Professor Joseph A. Maciariello and Professor Peter F. Drucker, along with the other faculty and participants in my decade of association with the university. I would like also to acknowledge the thousands of associates, peers, and managers in the organizations with whom I have had the pleasure of working these past five decades. To my family, who has been so supportive, I say thank you, Robert, Chris, Melinda, Cameron, Amanda, Dave, Michelle, Marcus, and Meredith. You are my team. P. T. Shank made this book a reality with her voice and creativity as well as hard work.

—Dr. Dean McKay

Many people helped me make this book happen. Specifically, I would like to thank H. Dean McKay for his business acumen; Ed and Mitchell, as always; Stephanie Sauls, for laundry, dinners, flowers, and generally being an amazing friend; Billy Taymor for his patience, humor, and being awake long after most people have gone to bed; Shoshanna Grossman, who saw me through the beginning of it; David Willis, who saw me through the end of it; and all my friends—both real and cyber—who understood and still love me.

—P. T. Shank

Introduction

When Dean and I first started talking about writing this book, we thought it would be very straightforward. We knew we wanted to take the language of business and translate it into plain English. He would choose the words, write the definitions, and take the role of business guru, ensuring the information was accurate. I would write the sentences, handle the technical part of writing a book, and take the role of target audience, ensuring the information was understandable. And we would have the next book in the excellent Words You Should Know series. To a certain extent, that is what happened. Over and over throughout the last year, Dean would present me with a definition, and I would say "But what does it mean?" until he had simplified it enough that even I could understand it. So it was straightforward. Dean has indeed chosen words and written definitions. I have written sentences. And you are reading this book. But something else happened as well. Once we started writing it, we came to realize it had far more potential than we originally recognized, and that was really exciting.

Yes, this book can be used in a very straightforward manner: When you hear a business word you don't understand, look it up and close the book. Easy. But it can be much more than that as well, depending on your needs.

Perhaps you need to know more about a concept than simply its definition and usage. An Internet search on "management style," for instance, turns up more than 200 thousand results! This book offers related words for each term. Combine a few of them in your search, and suddenly you are closer to finding the information you actually need.

Also, throughout the book, you will find boxes with further explanations of many of the defined words. While the definitions for these words are easy to understand, the concepts sometimes are not. The information found within the boxes will help clarify the concepts and how they apply to the business world.

We sincerely believe this book has become the valuable tool we always knew it could be. Hopefully, you will agree with us, whether you are well-established in an industry or just starting out. And who knows, maybe you'll even come to understand our excitement. We hope you do.

1

1-to-1 Marketing

Customizing the offering to the specific customer needs and desires. This process involves much more than just sales and marketing because the firm must be able to change how its products are configured or its service is delivered based on the individual needs of individual customers.

The technology company was successful because of its ability to offer 1-to-1 marketing to all its clients.

See also: Direct Marketing, End User

10Q Report

A financial statement filed with the U.S. Securities and Exchange Commission by a company, regarding its financial performance. This form is used for quarterly reports under Section 13 or 15(d) of the Securities Exchange Act of 1934. A quarterly report on this form must be filed within forty-five days after the end of each of the first three fiscal quarters of each fiscal year.

Investors and brokers are wise to track companies' 10Q reports before buying large amounts of stock.

See also: Financial Statement or Reports, Public Company, Quarterly Report, SEC Filings

10X Change

A strategic change from a current state, called X, to a future state in which the change is measured in orders of magnitude. This term refers to those rare moments when something creates a "10X change"—a change ten times greater than your average everyday change. Leadership believes in the exponential growth capacity of each team member. A 10X change is any change in a business environment that could potentially cause an industry change.

Business forecasters were aware that the creation of the personal computer would create a 10X change in the industry.

See also: Change, Change Management, Strategic Inflection Points

360-Degree Feedback

A means for leadership development; a method and a management tool that provides each employee the opportunity to receive performance feedback from his or her supervisor and four to eight peers, reporting staff members, coworkers, and customers.

Every year, the management staff received 360-degree feedback from their peers and staff in order to ensure a positive working environment for everyone in the department.

See also: Communications, Empowerment, Human Resources, Motivate, Performance Review

4 Ps of Marketing
Product, price, place (distribution), and promotion are the major marketing management decisions; these variables are known as the marketing mix.

Even though most customers may not be aware of it, nearly all decisions about buying products are based on the 4 Ps of marketing.

See also: Distribution, Marketing, Price, Product, Promotion

A

A-Team
An elite group or task force that is willing and able to solve difficult problems; a team that works together under uncertain conditions to create innovative solutions; a group having a special mission with a leadership role.

The new engineer was assigned to the A-team to tackle the division's most pressing problem.

See also: Leadership, Team Building, Teams

Abatement
A deduction in the amount of money owed.

The start-up received rent abatement to help them get things going in their production facility.

See also: Obligation, Payment in Kind

Ability
The quality of being able to perform; skill and aptitude that an employee needs in order to perform successfully the various tasks associated with a job; qualities that enable a person to achieve or accomplish something.

It is vital to hire someone based on his or her ability to perform the job at hand.

See also: Organization, Performance, Skill

Abstract
A document that summarizes and explains the important aspects of a larger, more detailed document.

The database contained many abstracts from articles on small business.

See also: Business Plan, Executive Summary

Accelerated Depreciation
Depreciation at a greater rate in the early years of an asset's life; an accounting method.

Due to the accelerated depreciation attached to some goods, many people recommend buying slightly used items over brand-new ones.

See also: Accounting, Depreciation, Taxes

Access
A process of inputting or retrieving data from a computer, network, or system.

The staff realized the computers were down when none of them could access the database.

See also: Computer, Data, Database, Network

Access Time
The time interval between a request for information and the start of the delivery process for a computer, network, or system.

Faster access time was one of the major selling points of the new computer system.

See also: Access, Computer, Float

Accessory Goods
Products used by business operations to function. Examples include computers, fax machines, office copiers, networks, and so on.

The small shop had a full inventory but the bare minimum of accessory goods needed to open for business.

See also: Administrative Expenses, Back Office, Operations

Accomplishment
The result of successfully meeting a goal; an achievement.

The award was given to the sales team for their accomplishment of increasing profits 20 percent over the estimated goal.

See also: Ability, Goals, Objectives, Success

Account
An organization's record of all the debits and credits chronologically posted to a ledger showing how each transaction affects a particular phase of a business. Entries are usually stated in monetary figures and reflect the current balances, if any.

A bookkeeper is often required to manage multiple accounts and track the strengths of all of them.

See also: Chart of Accounts, General Ledger, Ledger

Accountability
Taking responsibility for actions. An obligation to one's self—an obligation to lead a meaningful life, both in and out of the workplace, that is consistent with one's own values.

The CEO was impressed by the supervisor's sense of accountability for everything that happened in his department.

See also: Behavior, Governance, Responsibility

Accounting

The process of identifying, measuring, recording, and communicating financial information about a business or organization. Accounting information can be a helpful managerial and investment aid in the decision-making process.

The accounting firm was known and respected for the efficiency and uncompromising sense of integrity.

See also: Accounting Noise, Public Accounting, Purchasing Accounting

Accounting Noise

Complex rules that may affect the way a company's performance is related to the public. These rules do not affect the company's true performance, simply the way that performance is reported.

After a company has gone through a major change, it may be difficult for potential investors to cut through the accounting noise to discover how well the business is actually expected to perform.

See also: Accounting, Financial Statement or Report

Accounts Payable

Money or liabilities owed by a firm to vendor, suppliers, or service providers.

The secretary juggled the accounts payable so that the small firm's bills were paid every month within days of receiving the fees from their clients.

See also: Balance Sheet, Liability, Supplier, Vendor

Accounts Receivable

Money or liabilities due to a firm from customers for the purchase of inventory, goods, or services. Carried in the current-assets section of the firm's balance sheet.

The billing department sent out invoices on all accounts receivable that were not paid in full at the time of service.

See also: Assets, Balance Sheet, Customer, Inventories

Accounts Receivable Turnover

A measurement of how quickly customers pay their bills. The ratio of net credit sales to average accounts receivable.

Their bank asked for the accounts receivable turnover report to measure how quickly their customers paid their bills.

See also: Accounts Receivable, Credit, Financial Ratios, Turnover

Accrual-Based Accounting

An accounting method in which income is reported when earned and expenses are reported when an obligation is made rather than when money is received or paid.

Retail stores and other businesses that sell products and stock inventory use accrual-based accounting.

See also: Accounting, Bookkeeping, Expenses, Income

Accrue

Accumulate or increase over a period of time.

She chose to put her money into a CD rather than just into a savings account because interest would accrue at a faster rate.

See also: Depreciation, Expenses, Taxes

Accrued Expenses

Expenses yet to be paid; accumulated expenses in a given period that will be paid in the future.

It was agreed that the accrued expenses owed to the law firm would be paid at the end of the trial.

See also: Accrue, Expenses, Period

Accrued Interest

Interest yet to be paid; accumulated interest in a given period that will be paid in the future.

She opted to receive all accrued interest from her investments in one check at the end of the year.

See also: Accrue, Interest, Period

Accrued Taxes

Taxes yet to be paid; accumulated taxes that will be paid in the future.

The accountant tracked the accrued taxes in order to ensure there was enough cash to pay them when they came due.

See also: Accrue, Taxes

Accurate

Correct and exact; produces flawless work, generally as the result of pains-taking care.

The accountant was known for being detail oriented and accurate in every aspect of his job.

See also: Consistent, Quality

Acid Test Ratio

A ratio of current assets minus inventories, accruals, and prepaid items to current liabilities that is used to determine a firm's ability to meet current debt obligations.

According to the acid test ratio, the firm was actually in very good financial shape in spite of the unexpected quarterly losses.

See also: Assets, Liquid, Short-Term Debt

Acquisition

Acquiring control of a business or corporation.

The parent company's primary goal was to staff its new acquisition quickly and well before it began losing money.

See also: Due Diligence, Integration, Merger, Purchasing Accounting, Strategy

Acquisition Cost

The cost of purchasing equipment before sales tax.

The start-up bought much of its equipment slightly used in order to keep acquisition costs low.

See also: Capital Expenses (CapEx), Hard Assets

Acquittance

A receipt indicating payment in full, freedom from a financial obligation.

Every acquittance was kept on file in case questions arose later about the payment of the bills.

See also: Debt, Payments

Across the Board

Affecting all in an equal manner; comes from the New York Stock Exchange (NYSE) big board, a large board on which stock prices were once written, so when the majority of prices were up or down, the movement was shown "across the board."

Concern about the economy and rising prices cut consumer spending across the board, not just in the travel industry, over the summer.

See also: New York Stock Exchange (NYSE), Stock

Action Learning

A process in which a group of people come together more or less regularly to help each other to learn from their experience.

The company offered action learning programs as a way for senior management to lean on each other and junior management to receive mentoring.

See also: Action Plan, Group Processes, Teambuilding

Action Plan

A list of tasks that needs to be carried out in order to achieve a larger objective; may include other plans, activities, resources, and/or commitments.

> *The action plan was clear and concise so that everyone on the project knew what steps needed to be taken in order to achieve success.*

See also: Goals, Obstacles, Task

Actionable

An act, event, or occurrence that carries legal grounds for basing a lawsuit.

> *As offensive as the supervisor's statements and behaviors had been, her attorney told her they were, unfortunately, not actionable.*

See also: Arbitration, Audit

Activity List

A list of the defined activities that need to be completed for a project or task within an action plan.

> *The team was pleased that they had completed their activity list well enough in advance that the whole project moved forward sooner than expected.*

See also: Planning, Project, Task

Activity Sequencing

Identifying how activities affect each other and determining the best order to perform them in order to complete the project.

> *Although the committee's suggested activity sequencing seemed reasonable on paper, it didn't take into account ordinary delays expected by the technicians.*

See also: Program Evaluation and Review Techniques (PERT), Project, Time Management

Ad Hoc

A team, project, task force, or committee formed to address a specific issue or concern; singular-in-purpose effort; dealing with a particular organizational problem.

> *The CEO created an ad hoc committee to investigate the charges of harassment.*

See also: Organization, Project, Teams

Adaptation to Change

Methods and mechanisms that organizations use to react to internal and external environmental changes.

> *Businesses tend to survive longer when their adaptations to change are flexible, open-minded, and already in place prior to major market fluctuations.*

See also: Adapting, Change, Change Management, Organizations

Adapting
Capable of change from today's reality to a future state, such as change in response to new markets, globalization, and management changes.

Many nonprofit organizations had a hard time adapting to computerization in the 1980s and 1990s.

See also: Change, Flexible, Growth

Addendum
A supplement to a written document.

The actor requested that an addendum spelling out the specific needs of his staff be added to the contract.

See also: Appendix, Communication

Adhesion Contract
A contract that generally contains nonnegotiable terms that usually favor the party presenting it.

The band was known for the outrageous clauses in the adhesion contract they required each venue to sign before they agreed to perform.

See also: Contract, Letter of Intent (LOI), Terms

Adhocracy
A form of organization, usually with little or no structure, that allows for greater creativity and innovation around capturing opportunities, solving problems, and getting results.

Once the company moved from a bureaucracy to an adhocracy, several of the program directors had a hard time changing from a very controlling management style to one where staff was allowed more input and flexibility.

See also: Bureaucracy, Cross-Functional Team, Management, Organization, Teams

Adjustment
A debit or credit to a cardholder or seller's account to correct a transaction error.

When the woman's coat didn't arrive in the promised amount of time, the store made an adjustment on her credit card to reflect the removal of shipping charges.

See also: Accounting, Credit, Credit Card, Debt

Administrative Expenses

The expenses incurred in carrying out the activities listed in the management and organization section of the business plan.

The assistant secretary had to be laid off in order to cut back on administrative expenses.

See also: Accounting, Business Plan, Expenses, Income Statement

Administrivia

The day-to-day workings of an office environment required by administrators; Tasks that staff perform to maintain value in an organization that are needed to keep things going forward or to fulfill management needs.

The old secretary was invaluable to her boss because of her skill at dealing with administrivia.

See also: Administrative Expenses, Task

Advertising

A tool or management resource for increasing product differentiation and encouraging brand loyalty by communicating the features and benefits of a product/service through the use of radio, television, print, Internet, and other media.

Advertising is a large part of any company or product's success.

See also: Benefits, Brand, Communication, Marketing

Advertising-Based Model

A business model in which a firm generates revenue by charging advertisers for space (for example, in a magazine or on a Web site) or time (as in radio or TV).

The weekly neighborhood newspaper was able to stay in business once it switched over to an advertising-based model.

See also: Advertising, Business-to-consumer (B to C or B2C), Business Model, Revenue, Web Page

Advisory Board

A group of outside experts, typically three to six people, usually recruited by entrepreneurs to provide regular input and suggestions to management.

The entrepreneurs brought in an advisory board early in the planning stages of getting the new company up and running.

See also: Entrepreneur, Goals, Planning, Vision

Affiliate

An organization, firm, or other entity with a relationship with another company, peer, or larger entity.

Few people realized the community clinic was actually an affiliate of the nationally recognized hospital and was staffed by many of the same doctors.

See also: Control, Network, Relationships

Affinity Group

An organization made up of businesses (or representatives thereof) with common interests, such as an industry trade association or another group of entrepreneurs.

It is important for young professionals to find and join an affinity group that will assist them in becoming comfortable and growing in their chosen field.

See also: Trade Association

After-Hours Trading

Refers to stock trading that takes place outside the traditional trading hours of the major exchanges, such as the New York Stock Exchange (NYSE) and the NASDAQ Stock Market.

As more people use the Internet for investment purposes, after-hours trading is becoming more and more common.

See also: Stock, New York Stock Exchange (NYSE), Transactions

Aftermarket

The trading activity in a security immediately after its initial offering to the public; used to define the volatile time before prices stabilize or the secondary market for upgrades, such as the automotive non-factory parts.

Casual investors often wait until the aftermarket has settled down before deciding whether to invest in a specific stock.

or

Computer companies can make large sales based solely on the aftermarket when new technology that is desirable but not necessary becomes available.

See also: Capital Market, Initial Public Offering (IPO), Investor, Marketing, Security

Agenda

A list of items, issues, things to be considered; points to be discussed; outline of topics to be discussed in a meeting.

The agenda was so full, he wasn't sure if they would cover everything in the course of the hour-long meeting.

See also: Briefing, Kickoff Meeting, Meetings, Schedule

Aging of Receivables

An accounting method that provides management with information regarding a debt's age; or a method of estimating bad-debt losses by aging the accounts and then assigning a probability of collection to each classification.

The accountant urged the billing department to track outstanding fees because the aging of receivables indicated any accounts more than six months delinquent would be worthless.

See also: Accounts Receivable, Debt

Agreement

An understanding between two or more parties. May be formal or informal, legal or a "gentlemen's" agreement.

In many parts of the country, a handshake still creates as binding an agreement as a signed contract.

See also: Collective Bargaining, Confidentiality Agreement, Contract

Alert

Managers, executives, and employees who are observant and on the lookout. Aware, quick to understand the real importance and consequences of a situation or an occurrence.

The staff of the advertising department had to be alert to the changing values and morals of society in order to create effective campaigns.

See also: Human Resource, Observant

Allegiance

A commitment to a leader or organization that binds a party (intellectually or emotionally) to a course of action.

The business made it clear that its allegiance was to its customers and employees, even before that of the stakeholders.

See also: Commitment, Leadership, Loyalty, Stakeholders

Alliance

Any formal, inter-organizational, collaborative relationship with competitors or suppliers of complementary products and services aimed at avoiding crippling capital investments and gaining market entry or core competencies.

The owners of the start-up companies were excited about forming an alliance, secure in the knowledge that they could help each other grow.

See also: Collaborate, Relationship

Alpha Version

Development-stage terminology that expresses that the development of a piece of software is in its early stages and may require much further development. An alpha version of a program is also known as a "pilot" version, which can be tested for overall usability and training effectiveness.

Although the alpha version hadn't worked the way the designers had expected it to, the lessons learned from its failures were valuable in correcting the design flaws.

See also: Feasibility Study, Product Development

Ambitious

Intent on advancing, enterprising, having great desire and determination to achieve a certain goal. An advancement in position, authority, earnings, or reputation is usually the objective.

The plan to expand the company throughout the Northeast was ambitious, but management thought it could be done based on projected sales and growth.

See also: Energetic, Motivated

Ambivalence

Conflicting emotions or feelings about an individual, team, or organization; mixed feelings leading to uncertainty or indecisiveness.

The manager was ambivalent about his team's performance on the marketing campaign.

See also: Conflict, Indecisiveness, Leadership, Management, Uncertainty

Amortization

The allocation of a lump sum amount to different time periods. Either the paying off of debt in regular installments over a period of time or the deduction of capital expenses over a specific period of time.

Loan companies set up an amortization schedule that allows businesses to pay off their debts slowly so they don't go under but, at the same time, ensure the lender does indeed get its money back in a timely manner.

See also: Capital Investments, Debt, Installment

Analysis

The action of taking something apart in order to study it, such as financial analysis, competitive analysis, or strategic analysis.

The analysis of the competing firm's client list proved they were signing the clients everyone in town was hoping to bring on board.

See also: Competitive Analysis, PEST Analysis, Problem Solving, SWOT Analysis, Variance Analysis

Anchor Store or Client

A branded store or client that provides an attraction to draw new customers. The presence of such an anchor increases the market potential for other businesses and makes adjacent locations more desirable for entrepreneurs.

The mall closed within months after the two anchor stores moved out.

See also: Brand, Marketing

Angel Capital

Start-up money provided to entrepreneurs by friends, family, or wealthy individuals (often referred to as the 3 Fs: friends, family, and fools) whose motives may be non-monetary as well as financial.

The company's first round of financing was angel capital.

See also: Entrepreneur, Financing, Seed Capital, Venture Capital

Angels

Private investors, generally wealthy individuals who are former entrepreneurs or executives who invest in entrepreneurial companies.

The young businessmen wanted angels for the company, not just for the monetary assistance but for the advice and experience they would bring to the table.

See also: Advisory Board, Angel Capital, Incubator, Investor, Venture Capital

Animation

Effects used in presentations to improve the audience's experience; rapid sequential presentation of different graphics to create the illusion of motion.

Even the most engaging speakers can be more effective with the use of animation in their presentations.

See also: Presentation Slides, Visual Aid

Annual Percentage Rate (APR)

An interest rate that states the true cost of obtaining credit for the duration of the loan.

Even an APR that is only half a point lower than others can save a consumer a lot of money over the course of a loan.

See also: Credit, Interest, Loan

Annual Report

A document issued annually by public companies to their shareholders per Securities and Exchange Commission (SEC) regulations; includes information about a company's performance during the previous year, as well as management's view of the company's strategy for the future.

Serious investors will pay very close attention to a company's annual report before investing.

See also: 10K, Communication, Financial Statement or Report, Investors

Annual Sales

Sales or revenue received during the period of a year, before any expenses are deducted, for providing the firm's products and services.

In a weak economy, simply maintaining annual sales is often considered as much a success as increasing them would be in a strong economy.

See also: Income Statement, Revenue, Sales

Antitrust

Laws that prohibit agreements in restraint of trade, monopolization and attempted monopolization, anticompetitive mergers and tie-in schemes, and, in some circumstances, price discrimination in the sale of commodities. The antitrust laws apply to virtually all industries and to every level of business, including manufacturing, transportation, distribution, and marketing.

Antitrust laws were established to help ensure every company has the opportunity to succeed or fail on its own merits, without being held back by larger, already established businesses.

See also: Entry Barriers, Monopoly, Predatory Pricing

Appendix

An addition to the end of a document. In a business or feasibility plan, it may include copies of product/service information, legal agreements, resumes of principal owners, and so on.

Although people tend to ignore the appendix of a document, it often contains important, albeit secondary, information.

See also: Communication, Contract

Applicant

One who is seeking employment.

Employers appreciate having a large applicant pool because it tends to increase the chances of finding the right person for the position.

See also: Employ, Employee

Application

A form to be filled out by a job candidate when seeking employment, or the use of computer-based programs to process data for specific purposes.

Many companies have applications online, which allows people to apply for positions with ease.

or

Since the business world has become computerized, having a working knowledge of several different applications is beneficial to job applicants.

See also: Applicant, Applications Software, Data Processing

Application Service Provider (ASP)

Party that offers an outsourcing mechanism whereby it develops, supplies, and manages application software and hardware for its customers, thus freeing up customers' internal IT resources. The application software resides on the vendor's system and is accessed by users through a Web browser using HTML or by special-purpose client software provided by the vendor.

Using an ASP can be risky because if the vendor goes under or closes, information can be lost with very little, if any, warning to the customers.

See also: Client, Information Technology (IT), Server

Application Software

Software applications that are intended for end-users, such as database programs, word processors, and spreadsheets. Application software runs on top of system software.

Application software can often be purchased to upgrade a computer's capabilities.

See also: Application, Data Processing, Information Technology (IT)

Appraisal

A written document by a professional appraiser estimating the value or quality of an asset as of a given date or a performance evaluation of an employee.

It is important to get a fair appraisal prior to purchasing a big ticket item.
The company required yearly performance appraisals of all the employees.

See also: Employee, Promotion

Appraise

Estimating the value or determine the cost of an item or enterprise.

When the situation was appraised objectively, moving the company out of the city really was the best course of action in the long run.

See also: Appraisal, Valuation

Appreciation

An increase in the value of an asset.

The appreciation in property values expected in the neighborhood made buying even a small house an excellent investment.

See also: Assets, Capital Appreciation, Valuation

Appropriation

The application of the payment of a sum of money, made by a debtor to his creditor, to one of several debts as money that has been set aside by formal action to pay some known or anticipated costs.

The bookkeeper insisted on an accounting of the funds appropriated for each step of the loan repayment process because she feared the company was overreaching its financial abilities to pay back new loans.

See also: Creditor, Debt

Arbitrage

The opportunity to profit from a simultaneous purchase and sale of an asset; a rare and short-lived situation because market forces will close the gap between the purchase and sale prices, thus ending the opportunity.

The speculator realized she needed to take advantage of the arbitrage before the window of opportunity closed and the market prices equalized.

See also: Risk, Security

> **Arbitrage** is the opportunity to obtain a risk-free profit from the simultaneous purchase and sale of an asset, thus capturing the price differentials in similar or different markets. Such arbitrage opportunities are rare and short-lived as market forces will drive toward price convergence and eliminate such arbitrage opportunities.

Arbitration

A form of alternate dispute resolution in which a neutral third party hears the respective positions and renders a decision.

The contract disputes were eventually resolved when the company and the union were ordered into arbitration.

See also: Conflict Resolution, Mediation

Articles of Incorporation
A document filed with the secretary of state of the state of incorporation detailing things such as a company's purpose, powers under state law, classes of securities to be issued, and the rights and liabilities of directors and shareholders.

One of the first steps taken by a new business needs to be filing its articles of incorporation so that every step thereafter is legal.

See also: Board of Directors, Incorporate

Articulate
The ability to express oneself distinctly; able to speak effectively.

The CEO was disappointed to learn that as articulate as she had been during interviews, the new employee didn't have the skills or knowledge base to get the job done.

See also: Persuasive, Understanding

Artificial Intelligence (AI)
Using the power of a computer or network to improve the quality of management decisions, particularly complex strategic choices.

Many spam blockers use AI to filter out e-mail that is unsolicited, which in turn improves efficiency.

See also: Computers, Data Mining, Expert System, Fuzzy Logic, Strategic Choices

Asking Price
The price an owner places on an asset he is willing to sell. The asking price is also viewed as a benchmark price where the buyer and seller can begin negotiations since an agreed-upon price has yet to be reached.

During a housing boom, it is not uncommon for sellers to get above the asking price on a property.

See also: Benchmark, Bid Price

Aspirin Count Theory
A market theory that suggests that aspirin production and stock prices are inversely related, therefore when stock prices drop, aspirin production increases.

The aspirin count theory may be based on an old wives' tale but it certainly makes sense as well.

See also: Stock, Economics

Assertive

The ability and willingness to speak up without hesitation, make a position known; characterized by decided, often emphatic, statements and actions.

A good supervisor is able to juggle being assertive with diplomacy skills.

See also: Attitude, Positive

Assessment

An official estimate of the value of something for the purpose of computing property tax.

Based on the assessment, the house was worth far more than the young couple could afford to pay for it.

See also: Taxes, Valuation

Asset Lending

The loaning of money on the value of assets offered as security. The lender is protected from loss by the liquidation value of the assets.

Although she generally didn't like asset lending, the antiques presented as security were worth the risk she incurred by offering the couple the loan.

See also: Assets, Loan

Asset Redeployment

The strategic relocation of enterprise assets in order to increase profitability through improved competitive advantage.

The small company decided to try asset redeployment to help bring in more money so layoffs wouldn't be required.

See also: Assets, Competitive Advantage, Strategy

Asset Turnover

A company's total sales divided by its total assets. This ratio measures the overall efficiency with which a company uses its assets to produce sales. The higher the measure, the more efficient the business model.

The investors were pleased to see the asset turnover on the rise after three straight quarters of watching the ratio fall.

See also: Assets, Financial Ratios, Profit Margin, Revenue, Turnover

Asset-Based Financing

Financing an enterprise by using its hard assets for collateral to acquire a loan of sufficient size with which to finance operations.

Asset-based financing can be a safe or a risky choice depending on the strength of the company being taken over.

See also: Assets, Financing, Leveraged Buyout (LBO), Loan

Assets

Anything on a company's books considered as having a positive monetary value. Assets are reported on a firm's balance sheet.

Although the firm seemed financially secure, the accountants were beginning to become concerned about its dwindling assets.

See also: Balance Sheet, Return on Assets (ROA)

Assign

To transfer a right or interest to another person.

On his twenty-fifth birthday, the young man was assigned his half of his father's share in the business.

See also: Project, Resource

Assumptions

Factors that are believed to be true and affect business planning. Assumptions may impact risk and should always be documented and validated. Organizations make assumptions about many internal and external factors, including customers, competitors, industry evolution, regulation, technology, and the organization's resources, competencies, and cash flows.

Inaccurate assumptions about the dot-com industry led to the bubble bursting in the 1990s.

See also: Business Plan, Organizations, Resource

At-Will Employment

An employment policy that allows employees and employers to terminate the working relationship at any time.

Many seasonal and part-time employees are hired with an at-will employment understanding.

See also: Employee, Termination

Attrition

A reduction in the number of employees through retirement, resignation, or death.

Some downsizing may occur through attrition, while others take place more aggressively through layoffs and terminations.

See also: Downsizing, Employee, Retirement, Rightsizing

Audit
To examine an individual's or organization's records in an attempt to verify accuracy and legal compliance.

Insurance companies may audit clinic records at least once a year, provided they offer reasonable notice.

See also: Accounting, Adjustment, Due Diligence

Authentication
The process of confirming a user's identity; commonly done through the use of passwords or digital certificates.

Most credit card companies use security questions to ensure authentication of the caller.

See also: Authorization, Information Technology (IT), Password

Authority
Permission or approval to make decisions for team, organization, or firm; the power to command actions be taken; legitimacy to lead.

In order to be effective, managers need to have the authority to make decisions without double-checking with the CEO or president.

See also: Adhocracy, Delegation, Organizations

Authorization
Validating the authenticity of something or someone; approval of a bank card transaction by the card-issuing bank for a specified dollar amount.

Authorization is a critical step in processing credit cards for purchase of merchandise online.

See also: Authentication, Bank Card, Charge-Back, Credit, E-Commerce, Gateway, Power of Attorney, Sales Transaction

Average Annual Growth Rate
A measure of the rate of change in a firm's annual sales.

The average annual growth rate can indicate the overall health or weakness of a company.

See also: Net Worth, Revenue, Sales

Average Selling Price (ASP)
The average price for all items sold during a particular time frame, usually calculated for a specific category or a single seller's sales.

Online auctions benefit customers because products can be bought well below the ASP.

See also: Distribution, Price, Retailer

Award

A final decision that is rendered in favor of one party or something that is given on the basis of merit or need.

Many people believe there should be no upper limit to what juries may award victims in malpractice suits.

or

The team was thrilled to win the award, especially in light of the strength of the national competition.

See also: Grant, Honor

B

Baby Boomers

Consumers born from 1943 to 1960, characterized as experimental, individualistic, free spirited, social cause–oriented, distrustful of government, and generally cynical. As the largest generation cohort in America, they have dominated the market's attention and driven product development.

Many ad campaigns are directed toward baby boomers' reluctance to admit that they are aging.

See also: Cohort, Market Research, Marketing

Back Office

Administrative functions that support the processing of online transactions such as e-mail confirmations, shipping and tax calculations, packing slip creation, and report generation.

For every online store, there is someone in front of a computer handling back office issues.

See also: Administrivia, General and Administrative (G&A) Expenses, Overhead

Back Order

Part of an order that was not filled when the initial shipment was made.

Back orders are usually shipped when the items become available, without requiring the customer to place a reorder.

See also: Backlog, Customer

Back Pay

Wages that an employee is entitled to when the employer is found to be in violation of standard employment practices.

He received his back pay after going for an extended period of time without a paycheck.

See also: Employee, Wage

Backdating
Placing a date on a document that is prior to the date the document is actually drawn up; a process that makes a document effective from an earlier date.
Both parties agreed to backdate the contracts to the day they had first discussed the arrangement.
See also: Agreement, Contract, Stock Option

Backlog
Customer orders on products that are planned for shipment or delivery in the future.
The clerk was able to check the backlog and tell the customer when his equipment would be delivered.
See also: Back Order, Sales

Backup
A copy of a file or application that is kept separate from the original as a precaution against data loss in the event the original is lost or destroyed; or (two words) to make a copy of original work.
It is vital to keep a backup of all documentation stored on a hard drive.
or
He didn't back up the data, so we lost last week's work.
See also: Computer, Data, Data Recovery, Software

Bad Credit
The result of a company or individual being late or defaulting on bill payment.
He was concerned about qualifying for the loan because of the bad credit he had accrued while he was in college.
See also: Credit, Default

Bad Debt
Money that is still owed on an account and is past due; a debt that cannot be recovered.
Once the firm declared bankruptcy, its lenders had to write off their accounts as bad debt.
See also: Debt, Insolvency, Risk

Bailout Clause
A clause in a contract that allows a party to get out of the contract.
They decided to accept the bailout clause despite some reservations.
See also: Cancellation, Contract, Negotiation, Termination

B

Balance Sheet

A statement of the book value of a business, corporation, or individual at a particular date. The balance sheet provides a snapshot of the organization's assets, liabilities, and net worth or shareholder equity.

Her business acumen allowed her to interpret a company's balance sheet more accurately than most, so she knew what was a good investment even when others missed the opportunity.

See also: Assets, Financial Statement or Reports, Fiscal Year, Income Statement, Liability, Net Worth, Profit and Loss (P&L) Statement

Balanced Scorecard

A process that enables organizations to translate a company's vision and strategy into implementation by working from four perspectives: financial, customer, business process, and learning and growth. This not only allows the monitoring of present performance, the method also tries to capture information about how well the organization is positioned to perform in the future.

The balanced scorecard enabled the consultants to understand where the company wanted to go in the future and help its staff understand how to get there.

See also: Critical Success Factors (CSFs), Metrics, Organizations, Strategy, Teams, Vision

Bank

A financial institution; a commercial institution licensed as a receiver of deposits; a business for keeping, lending, exchanging and issuing money.

A bank-issued card that authorizes the holder to receive bank services and that often functions as a debit card is an important tool for any business.

See also: Bank Statement

Bank Card

A form of payment using either credit or debit from a bank account; any valid card issued by a card association or other card-issuing organization that is presented in payment for goods and services or to obtain cash advances.

Many people appreciate being able to use a bank card instead of having to carry cash.

See also: Bank, Credit Card

Bank Statement

A record of a firm's account that is regularly provided by the bank, either in print or online.

Our accountant reconciles the firm's bank statement each month.

See also: Bank, Cash Basis Accounting, Deposit Transactions

Bankruptcy

A state in which an entity is unable to meet its obligations and seeks court protection from its debtors. If the bankrupt entity is a firm, the ownership of the firm's assets is transferred from the stockholders to the bondholders. Shareholders are the last people to get paid if a company goes bankrupt. Secure creditors always get first grabs at the proceeds from liquidation. Also called Chapter 11.

The company decided to file for bankruptcy rather than to accumulate more debt and destroy its reputation even further.

See also: Assets, Creditor, Debt, Stockholder or Shareholder

Banner Ad

Internet advertising using graphics on a Web page to direct a viewer's attention to a product or service. Banners link to further information and Web pages.

The online store charged other businesses a small fee to have banner ads on its Web site.

See also: Advertising, Hyperlink, Internet, Web Page, World Wide Web (WWW)

Bar Chart

A schedule that shows project activities with associated start and completion dates.

The bar chart was posted where everyone involved with the project could see it and be sure to stay on target.

See also: Activity Sequencing, Business Plan, Critical Path Method (CPM), Gantt Chart, Milestone, Projects

Bar Code

An identifying mark made from a pattern of bars and spaces. A bar code is generated for individual items based on the item name/number or stock-keeping unit (SKU) on the item record.

If a bar code is ripped or missing, it can be difficult for clerks to find the price of an item.

See also: Inventories, Inventory Control, Retailer

Barrier

Conditions that create difficulty for an organization to meet a goal or objective; something that prevents progress or success toward an end.

There is a long-standing debate about how much of a barrier race and gender are in the corporate world.

See also: Entry Barriers, Obstacles

B

Barter

The exchange of one commodity for another without the exchange of money.

Although the project had very limited assets, the team met its goals through a barter arrangement.

See also: Commodity, Microeconomics

Baseline

The agreed-upon plan to which all subsequent plans will be compared for cost, schedule, and performance.

The initial product was so successful that everyone agreed it would be unfair to use it as a baseline for the projects that were scheduled to follow.

See also: Business Plan, Performance, Schedule

Basis

The cost or value of an asset as adjusted for tax purposes. Securities also have a basis, which is determined by the price an investor pays for the security plus any other incremental fees. The basis is then used to determine capital gains or losses for tax purposes when the stock is eventually sold.

She had bought stock at a high price, but because she had been given more shares as a gift, the basis was very reasonable.

See also: Capital Gains, Taxes

Behavior

A manner, action, or set of actions performed by a person under specified circumstances that reveal some skill, knowledge, or attitude; a way of conducting oneself.

The goal of training is to teach new employees the proper behavior in any situation, including unexpected or stressful ones.

See also: Attitude, Knowledge, Skill

Beliefs

Assumptions and convictions that a person holds to be true regarding people, concepts, or things; an organization's understanding of cause-effect relationships.

Many people choose to work for organizations that share their political, social, or environmental beliefs.

See also: Behavior, Convictions, Mindset, Organizations

Benchmark

A standard of reference used for comparison; a process of comparing practices within a company to the very best practices in some of the very best organizations, within and outside the industry; a process for measuring "best practice" performance and comparing the results to corporate performance in order to identify opportunities for improvement.

The overwhelming success of the holiday ad campaign was the benchmark by which all other campaigns would be measured.

See also: Competitive Advantage, Core Competencies, Metrics, Strategy

Benefits

A collection of advantages; solutions offered to customers through a company's products/services; the advantages that are inherent in a product/service or that customers expect to receive and that motivate customers to purchase it.

An effective ad campaign communicates the benefits of buying a specific product well enough that consumers believe they need the product.

See also: Communication, Marketing, Sales

Bid

An offer of money in exchange for an item that is for sale.

Once the national chain made a bid for the shops, the medium-sized businesses dropped out because they knew they couldn't match the prices the larger company could offer.

See also: Asking Price, Bid Price

Bid Price

A price offered by a prospective buyer to begin the negotiation process of buying a security or business asset.

Although the firm had been in his family for years, the man was tempted by the increasingly high bid prices being offered by the competitors.

See also: Bid, Negotiation

Big, Hairy, Audacious Goals (BHAGs)

A goal, vision, or plan that causes the organization to stretch to obtain the result; a challenge by leadership to an organization to fulfill a mission or strategy.

By setting BHAGs, companies often accomplish far more than if they had set goals that would be expected to be met easily.

See also: Catalytic Mechanisms, Goals, Strategy

B

Bill of Sale
A written agreement stating the terms by which ownership of goods is transferred to another party.

It is wise to get a bill of sale for any large purchase item you cannot simply carry away.

See also: Agreement, Term Sheet

Bit
The fundamental informational building block used by all computers. A bit is a single character in a binary number.

The digital camera images contained 3 million bits of information.

See also: Computer, Data, Information

Blog
A journal that is available on the Web; frequently updated, chronological entries on a particular topic. This word was created from the combination of the words "Web log."

These days, teenagers are as likely to host a blog in order to keep in touch with their friends as they are to use the phone.

See also: Communication, Internet, Link, Media, Web Page, World Wide Web (WWW)

Board of Directors
A group of people elected by a corporation's shareholders to oversee the management of the company. A board often consists of executive and non-executive directors. Executive directors play an active part in running the company, while non-executive directors are there to offer advice.

The program supervisors reported to the board of directors on a quarterly basis.

See also: Chairman of the Board (COB), Chief Executive Officer (CEO), Strategy

Bonds
Debt securities that pays the holder a fixed sum on a regular schedule for a fixed term. Bonds are issued by corporations and governments; they come in a wide variety of types.

In the past, the United States government has issued war bonds in order to maintain a cash flow during wartime.

See also: Debt, Security

Bonus

A sum of money or equivalent incentives given to employees in addition to base compensation. Bonuses can also come in the form of extra vacation time, gifts, and other nonmonetary awards.

Even when business was slow, the store owner made sure his staff received holiday bonuses to show his appreciation for their hard work.

See also: Compensation, Intangible Rewards, Perquisite or Perk Rewards

Book Inventory

The balance of the inventory account after all incoming inventory is added and the cost of outgoing goods is subtracted.

The book inventory type of perpetual inventory system is usually verified annually by taking a physical inventory and reconciling any discrepancies.

See also: Accounting, Inventories

Book Value

The value of an asset as reflected in the books of the company owning the item.

The book value of the items at auction could never accurately represent the sentimental value several of the pieces had to the buyers.

See also: Accounting, Assets, Balance Sheet, Liability, Net Worth

Book-to-Bill Ratio

A measure of sales trends of a company or overall industry. The ratio divides the amount of new orders "booked" by the value of the products shipped each month (or "billed").

The strength of the technology industry can be measured in part by watching the book-to-bill ratio every month.

See also: Ratio Analysis, Revenue, Sales

Bookkeeper

A person who records the accounts or transactions of a business in a general ledger.

The store owner hired a bookkeeper to handle finances when she opened her second shop.

See also: Accounting, General Ledger

Bookkeeping

B

The practice or profession of recording the accounts and transactions of a business through a systematic and convenient record of money transactions in order to show the condition of a business enterprise.

Having an accurate and trustworthy bookkeeping staff is vital to the success of any large business.

See also: Accounting, Bookkeeper

Bookmark

A marker or address that identifies a Web site or Web page. Most Web browsers allow users to save and organize bookmarks as a convenient way to mark Web sites for future reference.

Most browsers have a section called "favorites" where users can bookmark their favorite sites for easy access.

See also: Application Software, Web Page, World Wide Web (WWW)

Boom

A period when business expands and the economy experiences rapid growth and rising prices. During such a period, there is an increased demand for goods and services and unemployment rates fall.

The boom that resulted after the election showed the country's faith in the new president's economic policies.

See also: Demand, Economics, Leading Indicators

Boot Camp

An indoctrination program in some aspect of leadership or management; going to such a program means being immersed in a discipline or topic with a group or team of cohorts.

The board recommended everyone on the management team attend boot camp on cultural differences before the expansion into Europe took place.

See also: Leadership, Teams

Bootstrapping

A management approach that uses internal methods to generate money to be used for a proposed project or venture; a low start-up, pay-as-you-go approach to launching businesses.

Many managers believe that bootstrapping rather than waiting until a new company has more than enough start-up monies helps create a sense of excitement and energy that bonds the staff and makes the company stronger in the long run.

See also: Seed Capital, Start-Up, Venture Capital

Boston Consulting Group Box (BCG Box)

A framework for analysis and communication strategy for a business with a portfolio of products, services, programs, strategic business units or companies.

The consultants used a BCG Box to present the analysis of the programs.

See also: Cash Cow, Competitive Advantage, Dog, Harvest, Strategic Business Unit (SBU), Strategy

Bottleneck

Anything that slows down or impedes by creating an obstruction or that halts the progress or flow of an activity, process, or operation in an organization.

The computer glitch caused a bottleneck throughout the entire production line.

See also: Barriers, Obstacle

Bottom-Up

An estimating technique in which every activity is individually estimated and then added together to determine the total project estimate.

Each department was required to provide the CEO and the treasurer with a bottom-up budget every year.

See also: Budget, Business Plan, Decentralized, Organizations, Planning, Structure

Bottom Line

The line in a financial statement that shows net income or loss. Based on the bottom figure on a profit-and-loss statement, it refers to an organization's most important measure of success: profits.

Even established businesses must keep an eye on the bottom line in order to continue to be successful.

See also: Income Statement, Loss, Profit, Valuation

Brainstorming

A management technique used to foster ideas, solve problems, set goals, establish priorities, and make assignments for employee accomplishments. As a semi-structured creative group activity, this method is used most often in ad-hoc business meetings to come up with new ideas for innovation or improvement.

The committee came up with several good fundraising ideas in one brainstorming session.

See also: Creativity, Innovation

Brand

The symbolic embodiment of key information that differentiates a product or service from the competition. Brands matter because companies act just like people when it comes to evaluating what products or services to buy.

Many teenagers can identify popular brands faster than they can identify current world leaders.

See also: Brand Equity, Brand Loyalty, Brand Management, Customer Loyalty, Marketing, Value Proposition

A **brand** and **branding** today is a strategic tool that helps the supplier cut through the morass of the market, get noticed, and connect with the customer on many levels and in ways that matter. Consumers are drawn to **brands'** irrational benefits (status, prestige, affinity, self-security). Business customers specify and purchase based on rational drivers (pricing, product performance, metrics).

Brand Equity

The total or intrinsic value of a brand. Awareness of a firm's products or services are measured by consumer goodwill, loyalty, and differentiation in the marketplace.

The brand equity of the fast-food chain kept it afloat until changes could be made based on the negative documentary.

See also: Brand, Brand Loyalty, Brand Management, Customer Loyalty, Marketing, Value Proposition

Brand Loyalty

A consumer's commitment to repurchase the same brand of product he or she has bought before. Customers have a strong, positive attitude toward the brand which is then exhibited through repurchase behavior.

As amusing as it may seem, arguments have actually occurred between customers because of disagreements about brand loyalty.

See also: Advertising, Brand, Loyalty

Brand Management

Management of the process for shaping the image of a product, service, or business in the marketplace.

Weakening sales can often be corrected with shrewd brand management.

See also: Brand, Brand Loyalty, Customer Loyalty, Marketing, Value Proposition

Break-Even

The level of sales at which total revenue equals total costs incurred; the point at which the venture is meeting expenses with no profit and no loss. The break-even point in units equals total fixed cost divided by unit price less unit variable cost.

Few new businesses reach the break-even point in their first year in operation.

See also: Fixed Cost, Loss, Profit, Variable Cost

Bricks and Clicks

An integration of both online and traditional business models. A "bricks and clicks" business uses both a traditional business model and an Internet model and thus has dual channels of distribution and customer experiences, face-to-face and e-commerce.

The bricks-and-clicks strategy has been adopted by retailers who want to be available to customers who don't live nearby shopping centers.

See also: Bricks and Mortar, Business Model, Clicks and Mortar, E-Commerce

Bricks and Mortar

The business model employed by traditional companies that have yet to embrace the Internet as a means of serving customers; these businesses offer only face-to-face consumer experiences.

Many bricks-and-mortar companies are smaller, mom-and-pop businesses.

See also: Business Model, Clicks and Mortar, E-Commerce

Bridge Loan

A short-term, temporary method of financing that is used until permanent financing can be secured.

The entrepreneurs were happy to accept a bridge loan until the business was strong enough for a bank to take a chance on them.

See also: Financing, Loan

Briefing

A concise presentation that is given in context, consisting of facts, data, information, analysis, conclusions, and strategy. A communications art used by and for executives to impart critical data for decision making.

As a good presenter, she realized that whenever she gave a briefing, she was not just offering facts but was also selling a whole concept.

See also: Communication, Information, Presentation Slides

Broker

B

An intermediary who manages a sale and purchase, usually compensated through a success fee upon completion of the transaction.

After unsuccessfully trying to sell their house on their own, the couple hired a broker to manage the sale.

See also: Buyer, Security

A **broker** earns a commission, or brokerage, when the contract of sale has been made, regardless of whether the contract is satisfactorily executed. The **broker** is paid by the party that started the negotiation. In practice, merchants and other salespeople act as **brokers** at times.

Bubble

A period characterized by speculation and rapid expansion, in which values are considered overpriced. Once a bubble is "burst," prices and values fall dramatically. Bubbles occur in the markets such as stocks, commodities, and housing.

Many investors were stuck with properties in undesirable locations when the housing bubble burst.

See also: Assets, Boom, Economics

Budget

Planned revenues and expenses for a given time period, usually drawn up annually for the purpose of allocating resources and making informed business decisions.

Although paychecks are accounted for in budgets, bonuses may not be so they are usually given out sparingly in order to prevent the company from ending up in the red.

See also: Business Plan, Operating Budget, Variance

Bulk

Large quantities; buying or selling a product in large quantities to secure or provide a discount.

Savings-and-loan institutions accept savings deposits and invest the bulk of the funds they receive in mortgages.

See also: Discount Rate, Quantity Discount

Bullet Points

Key ideas or phrases used in presentations and executive summaries for emphasis.

The agenda listed bullet points that would be discussed in depth during the meeting.

See also: Communication, Flipchart, Presentation Slides

Burden of Proof

An obligation of a firm's management to prove or disprove certain facts.

The burden of proof was on the CEO to show the board that the project was still viable.

See also: Management, Obligation

Bureaucracy

An organization that is driven by structure, hierarchy, and trivia. Because the structured organization takes precedence, opportunities get missed, crucial issues go unresolved, and efforts to change usually get nipped in the bud. Reward systems in most companies—salaries, bonuses, options—are typically tied to an employee's box in the bureaucracy.

The exchange of information is practically nonexistent in a bureaucracy, so many good ideas never get to the right people.

See also: Adhocracy, Organizations

Burn Rate

A metric for reporting negative cash flow in a start-up enterprise. An increase or decrease in burn rate is usually related to spending for staff to create products or open channels to market.

When sales fell dramatically short of what was expected, the company had to reduce the burn rate by laying off several staff members.

See also: Cash Flow, Metrics, Start-Up, Venture Capital

Business Angels

High-net-worth individuals, friends, or family who provide start-up funds to entrepreneurs for financial as well as nonmonetary motives.

Every year, the firm threw a lavish "thank-you" party for its business angels.

See also: Angels, Seed Capital

Business Broker

An intermediary person/agent who buys and sells businesses for other people.

The new hire is a good business broker because he is able to work with both buyer and seller to close a deal.

See also: Acquisition, Broker

Business Concept

The theory or definition that an enterprise is based upon, including assumptions about the environment of the organization, structure, market, the customer, purpose, technologies employed, mission, and core competencies needed to achieve the mission and purpose.

The CEO ensured his entire staff, from management to the hourly workers, understood the company's business concept.

See also: Assumptions, Competitive Advantage, Core Competencies, Mission, Purpose, Risk

Business Cycle

The ebb and flow of the economy or a sector. The five stages of the business cycle are peak, recession, trough, recovery, and expansion.

Analysts watch economic trends in order to predict and prepare for the next business cycle downturn.

See also: Economics, Inflation

Business Ecosystems

The network of businesses and organizations that an enterprise affects and is affected by in serving its markets, customers, and communities. These networks include suppliers, distributors, outsourcing firms, makers of related products or services, technology providers, and a host of other organizations.

From their earliest days, Wal-Mart and Microsoft—unlike companies that focus primarily on their internal capabilities—have realized globalization is revolutionizing the way manufacturers operate and pursued strategies that not only aggressively further their own interests but also promote their business ecosystems' overall health.

See also: Globalization, Organizations, Outsourcing, Value Chain

Business Ethics

The moral obligation placed on business leaders, management, and employees of an organization to be honest and fair in their dealings with all stakeholders of the organization.

University business programs offer classes in business ethics in order to stress the importance of having integrity on the professional level.

See also: Corporations, Governance, Leadership, Stakeholders

Business Intelligence

A business planning process that fulfills strategic management needs to know what is going on in markets and sectors where the firm competes; to understand the implications of market factors relevant to the business; and to understand how a business model represents an improved solution to the problem, challenge, or opportunity a strategy addresses. The goal of this process is for members of an organization to know how to produce the product or service in sufficient quantities and of sufficient quality to create appropriate prices and to market the product in such a way as to effectively transform customer information into revenues—customer data converted to profits.

In today's corporate world, new employees must have the business intelligence to compete within their chosen industry, not just the skills to perform their jobs on a day-to-day basis.

See also: Business Model, Business Plan, Competition, Market Factors, Strategic Management

Business License

A permit to conduct business; certification that local and state governments require businesses to obtain and post; an adherence to regulations or law.

The winery was required to have both federal and state business licenses in order to produce and ship its product.

See also: Permit

Business Literacy

Ability to read and write the language of business in order to speak with and to businesspersons. Fundamental to an individual's ability to solve or dissolve problems at levels of proficiency necessary to function on the job, in an organization, or in the marketplace.

After dealing with the regulations and legalities of opening her own salon, the woman felt she had been given a crash course in business literacy.

See also: Communications, Financial Literacy

The link between reading ability and employability has long been common knowledge. A multiyear, international study of **business literacy** found that not only does a person's **business literacy** level mean the difference between employment and unemployment, it can also be the deciding factor between good or poor health and can even influence how well that person's children will do in life.

Business Model

A method or description of how an enterprise functions; a general template that describes the enterprise's major activities. Used in combination with strategy to guide a firm's major decisions.

Implementing the business model proposed by the consultants would require a change in attitude and business practices on the part of just about every member of the organization.

See also: Business Plan, Competitive Advantage, Decision Making, Strategy

Business Philosophy

The unique outlook, insight, and mindset an entrepreneur, owner, or manager takes toward the conduct of business, the creation of customers, and service to its stakeholders.

The business philosophy of the shop stressed customer comfort and satisfaction over the elite, high-end atmosphere most stores on the street embraced.

See also: Mission, Purpose, Stakeholders, Strategy, Values, Vision

Business Plan

A document that provides the objectives of a business and the steps necessary to achieve those objectives. Provides focus and direction to move a firm from today's realities to a future vision along a path that includes operations, marketing, sales, control systems, management philosophy, and growth plan.

Part of writing an effective business plan is understanding why a company's customers make the decisions they do.

See also: Competitive Landscape (Environment), Goals, Investment, Milestone, Objectives, Operations, Profit, Strategy, Vision

Business Proposal

A communication to a customer or client for a product or service; a bid for business, whether solicited or unsolicited. An answer to potential customers' questions that is crafted to persuade them to become customers in fact.

The well-written business proposal won over the audience in spite of their initial reluctance to be involved with the project.

See also: Client, Communication, Customer, Solutions

Business-to-Business (B-to-B or B2B)

Transactions between businesses; an Internet strategy that uses e-commerce to create and service business customers.

The rising popularity of Internet businesses and e-marketplaces has resulted in very lucrative B2B partnerships for many online venues.

See also: Business-to-Consumer (B-to-C or B2C), E-commerce, Internet

Business-to-Consumer (B-to-C or B2C)

Transactions between business and consumers directly; an Internet strategy using e-commerce to create and service consumers.

Because it frequently removes the middleman, the Internet has created more B2C businesses than at any time in the past.

See also: Business-to-Business (B-to-B or B2B), E-Commerce, E-Tailer, Internet

Buy-In

When people, teams, groups, and organizations embrace a concept, strategy, or action. The process of getting buy-in involves obtaining commitment to a goal or project; giving the participants a stake in the outcome.

The sales team was so strong they were able to get buy-in for the new business from even the most reluctant principals.

See also: Commitment, Goals, Leadership, Motivation, Teams

Buy-Sell Agreement

Provisions for selling a business that are usually agreed upon by business associates, setting terms for which associates can buy out the others.

When the senior partner brought in a junior partner, they signed a buy-sell agreement to cover transfer of the business when the older man retired.

See also: Agreement, Partnership, Stockholder or Shareholder

Buyer

A person whose work is purchasing merchandise for resale; a firm or group that buys another business, product, or service.

As a buyer for a major department store, the woman made sure that her clothing was always on the cutting edge of fashion.

See also: Acquisitions, Buyer Bargaining Power, Client, Economic Buyer, Seller

Buyer Bargaining Power

The influence buyers have over the competitors in a given industry by creating and controlling the demand for given products and services.

When the soft-drink company changed its formula, buyer bargaining power forced it to return to the old flavor.

See also: Competitive Advantage, Porter's Five-Force Model, Strategy

C

C Corporation

A business organization in which the owners are taxed separately from the business.

The profits expected by the owners and investors dictated a C corporation structure.

See also: Incorporate, S Corporation, Taxes

Callback

A situation during which the originator of a call is immediately called back in a second call as a response. Web Callback is a technology that allows a customer to enter a telephone number in a form on a company Web site. The company gets the Web Callback request, and a call center agent calls the customer back on the number entered.

The callback feature improves customer service by allowing customers to continue their work while awaiting the return phone call rather than having to sit and wait on hold.

See also: E-Commerce, Web Page

Campaign

A series of marketing efforts, such as e-mail, phone, direct mail, or printed advertisements, used to generate business.

The new store launched a major campaign announcing its grand opening and offering discounts to anyone presenting a flier or email coupon.

See also: Customer Relationship Management (CRM), Marketing

Cancellation

Termination of an agreement or contract.

The inspection of the house went so badly that the sellers agreed to the cancellation of the contract presented by the buyers.

See also: Agreement, Contract

Cancellation Fee

A fee imposed for breaking a service contract.

Most cell phone service providers charge a cancellation fee for discontinuing service before the initial contract expires.

See also: Cancellation, Contract, Fee

Candid

Truthful, sincere, straightforward expression; impartial. People with this characteristic have the ability to say what is on their mind.

Although some people appreciated his candid nature, it often caused him problems in dealing with office politics.

See also: Integrity, Leadership

Cannibalization

A company's introduction of a new part, product, or service that draws customers and sales away from a current, pre-existing part, product, or service.

Many companies will discontinue old lines before offering new ones in order to prevent cannibalization between products.

See also: Market Share, Marketing, Product Development, Revenue, Sales

Capable

Extremely competent; having the ability and/or resourcefulness to accomplish an objective.

Our sales team is extremely competent and capable of meeting its targets.

See also: Ability

Capacity

The ability to perform or produce a desired output; the capability of a worker, system, or organization to produce output per time period.

The improved capacity of the assembly line allowed the toy company to keep up with the demand caused by the popularity of the new cartoon character.

See also: Ability, Organizational Capacity, Productivity

Capital

A synonym for cash. Capital is cash held in a checking or savings account. Also goods, material assets, equipment, machinery, or tools.

The entrepreneurs were willing to work menial jobs in order to accumulate the capital they needed to launch their own business.

See also: Capital Asset, Capital Market, Cash

Capital Asset

Assets intended for long-term use by a business, such as land, building, or production facilities, the use of which creates more capital for the business. Capital assets are reported on a company's balance sheet and are depreciated for tax purposes.

The firm listed several apartment buildings as capital assets on its taxes.

See also: Balance Sheet, Capital, Capital Gains, Depreciation, Real Property

Capital Expenses (CapEx)

Business spending on additional plant equipment and inventory, such as physical assets, buildings, and computers. Similar to depreciation, it is a means of measuring the consumption of the value of long-term assets like equipment or buildings.

The company's capital expenses dropped dramatically once it was able to relocate all the satellite offices into one large building downtown.

See also: Basis, Depreciation, Financial Statement or Reports, Fixed Asset

Capital Gains

Profits from the sale of assets; appreciation of an asset. Determined by subtracting the purchase price from the selling price.

During a housing boom, sellers can expect high capital gains from the sale of their properties.

See also: Capital Asset, Profit, Purchase Price, Taxes

Capital Investments

A term applied to investment funds used to purchase items like manufacturing equipment and real estate.

The stylist rented a chair at the local salon until she made capital investments necessary to buy a small storefront and open her own shop.

See also: Capital, Investment

Capital Market

Financial market where debt or equity securities are traded; a source of capital for businesses.

The entrepreneurs increased the money from the small loan on the capital markets in order to fund their latest venture.

See also: Capital, Equity, Security

Cardholder

A person or entity that is issued a credit or debit account that is accessed through the use of a card.

Even though his parents made him a cardholder on one of their accounts for emergency purposes, he often used the card to pay for parties instead.

See also: Credit, Debit

Career

The sequence of jobs occupied by a person through the course of his or her lifetime. The concept of a career is shifting from a closed set of achievements, like a chronological resume of past jobs, to a defined set of pursuits looking forward.

Being hired as the anchor for a major news program was the perfect culmination of her long career in journalism.

See also: Mentor, Skill

Carrying Charge

Premium rates charged on overdue accounts.

Many people do not realize that they will incur a carrying charge as well as the normal interest if they do not pay their credit card bills on time.

See also: Finance Charge, Interest

Carrying Cost

Cost incurred from storage of inventory.

The small store kept a minimum of stock on hand in order to minimize the carrying cost.

See also: Inventories, Turnover

Cartel

A group of independent business organizations that band together in an attempt to limit competition by influencing prices, production, and marketing.

Since the United States' economy is based on capitalism, cartels are illegal because they hold back free trade.

See also: Monopoly, Oligopoly, Organizations

Cash

Liquid assets with fixed values, including currency, checks, money orders, and traveler's checks, that may be deposited in a bank. Reported on a firm's balance sheet as a current asset.

Most large businesses deal in stocks and shares rather than making large deals in cash.

See also: Balance Sheet, Cash Equivalents, Current Assets, Liquid

Cash-Basis Accounting

An accounting method that immediately records the receipt of cash or the expense for goods and services. This is not an accepted method of bookkeeping for publicly held companies.

Cash-basis accounting is sometimes used by small service companies that don't deal in inventories and keep accounting records only for cash receipts and cash payments.

See also: Accounting, Bank Statement, Chart of Accounts, Ledger

Cash Cow

A product or service that sells very well and has a low cost. The name implies the relative ease with which cash is obtained—like milking a cow.

Coffee drinks were considered the café's cash cow because they cost so little to make and could be sold for $2 or $3 a cup.

See also: Cash Flow, Strategy

Cash Discount

An incentive offered to customers to pay promptly; a discount given to the buyer as an incentive to render immediate payment or payment within a specific time frame.

The furniture store offered a 10 percent cash discount to anyone who paid in full at the time of purchase.

See also: Credit, Discount, Incentive

Cash Equivalents

Liquid assets, convertible to cash; reported on the balance sheet as a current asset. Includes funds invested in U.S. Treasury Bills, money market accounts, and other investments with a maturity of three months or less when purchased.

All of her funds were cash equivalents instead of in long-term investments because her paychecks were so sporadic.

See also: Balance Sheet, Liquid

Cash Flow

Cash generated, or burned, from company operations, prior to depreciation, amortization, and other non-cash charges; the most important consideration of business survival.

Since he remembered the lean years and eating sandwiches at his desk, the senior partner warned the whole firm to mind the cash flow almost on a weekly basis.

See also: Burn Rate, Cash Flow Statement

Cash Flow Statement

A report that details how a company's cash position has changed during a period of time. One of three parts of a firm's financial statement that shows how changes in balance sheet and income accounts affected cash and cash equivalents. This statement breaks the analysis down according to operating, investing, and financing activities.

Although companies need a person who dreams big in order to grow, they also need a person who keeps a close eye on the cash flow statement.

See also: Cash Flow, Financial Statement or Reports

Cash on Delivery (COD)

Payment that is made when a purchase is delivered.

Due to late payments, the auto parts store required cash on delivery from the garage for any orders it placed.

See also: Cash Sales, Delivery

Cash Ratio

A measure of the extent to which a business can liquidate assets and cover short term liabilities; used by short-term creditors. Calculated by adding the cash and cash equivalents and dividing by current liabilities.

The firm's cash ratio was sufficient to handle their need to finance inventory for the holiday season.

See also: Current Ratio, Financial Ratios, Liquid

Cash Sales

A transaction that records the sale of goods or services for which immediate payment is received. A cash sale is entered when payment for goods or services has been received at the time of delivery.

Although the small store took credit cards, almost all of its transactions were cash sales.

See also: Retailer, Sales

Catalytic Mechanisms

A means of producing desired results in unpredictable ways. Catalytic mechanisms have the following characteristics and benefits. They distribute power for the benefit of the overall system; they put a process in place that all but guarantees that the vision will be fulfilled; they help organizations to get the right people in the first place; they produce an ongoing effect.

The team came up with catalytic mechanisms that, while unexpected by the department, resulted in a more successful project than predicted.

See also: Organizations, Process, Results, Vision

Certified Check

A check guaranteed to be good by the bank on which it is drawn. In order to eliminate the risk of covering the check, many banks charge the depositor's account immediately for the amount of the check.

In order to get the transaction completed on schedule, a certified check was sent overnight to assure the seller that the money was available.

See also: Bank, Cash, Cash Equivalents, Payments

Certified Public Accountant (CPA)

An accountant who has met all of a state's requirements and has received a state certificate.

Most companies use a CPA to perform their annual audits and to prepare their tax reports.

See also: Accounting, Audit

Chairman of the Board (COB)

The leader of a firm's board of directors. Elected by the other board directors.

The chairman of the board called the meeting to order once everyone had gotten coffee and was settling down.

See also: Board of Directors, Top Management

Change

Transition from same to different; adapting to a new state, structure, or strategy.

Some of the old guard had difficulty adjusting to the change the young CEO brought to the company with his new ideas and philosophies.

See also: Change Management, Organizations, Strategy, Uncertainty

Change Management

The practice of reinventing, steering, or reengineering a company in a new strategic direction and keeping all involved people and projects aligned with the new goals as the organization, jobs, technology, and processes are uprooted.

The program director understood part of her job was the change management that would help her staff stay current.

See also: Change, Culture, Leadership, Organizations, Reengineering, Strategy

Change Request

A document that is submitted to request a change to any part of the project management plan after the plan is approved.

The techs submitted a change request once they realized the original settings planned for the software would not hold up under real world application.

See also: Configuration Management, Project, Project Management

Channel Stuffing

A practice of inflating sales in a period by forcing more products through a given distribution channel than the channel is capable of selling in the period.

Manufacturers pressure distributors by channel stuffing to take inventory to bolster their revenues and smooth out demands for products in the marketplace.

See also: Accounts Receivable, Distribution Channel, Inventories

Chaordic Organizations

An organization that can move from order to temporary chaos and back again without crisis; a form that facilitates connection and collaboration among members, teams, and groups; anything simultaneously orderly and chaotic.

Often, chaordic organizations are better equipped to handle sudden shifts in the marketplace because they are more used to dealing with the unexpected.

See also: Adhocracy, Chaos, Collaboration, Organizations, Relationships, Teams

Chaos

Unpredictability; complex, dynamic, nonlinear, co-creative and far-from-equilibrium systems and organizations; the result of too much change too fast.

The board's goal was to make the transition during the merge as smooth as possible, thus minimizing chaos and setbacks.

See also: Chaordic Organizations, Crisis, Entrepreneurial Chaos, Unpredictability

Character

A distinguishing feature; a complex of mental and ethical traits marking a person or a group or a team; attributes that determine a person's moral and ethical actions and reactions.

He was respected not only for his business acumen but for his uncompromising character as well.

See also: Behavior, Integrity

Charge-Back

Credit that a merchant is compelled to issue to a cardholder's account electronically. When a customer does not receive a paid-for item, credit is initiated and the payment to the merchant is reversed.

Once the purchase was proven to be a fraudulent transaction, the store immediately issued a charge-back to the customer.

See also: Bank, Cardholder, Credit Card

Chart of Accounts

A list of accounts that make up a firm's accounting system and provide management with the information needed to make good business decisions. Contained in the general ledger and including asset, liability, equity, revenue, and expense accounts.

The accountants presented the director with the chart of accounts at the monthly financial meeting.

See also: Accounting, Accounts, General Ledger

Chief Executive Officer (CEO)

Highest-ranking corporate officer who provides leadership for the enterprise; appointed by the board of directors.

One of the reasons he was a good CEO was that he took his responsibility to his employees as seriously as his responsibility to the stockholders.

See also: Leadership, Top Management

Chief Financial Officer (CFO)

The corporate executive responsible for the financial planning and tracking of a company; member of the executive team who represents the firm in the financial world.

The new CFO knew she was going to have to repair the company's reputation after the scandal caused by her predecessor.

See also: Leadership, Top Management

Chief Operating Officer (COO)

An executive who oversees the day-to-day operations of a company.

The COO took pride in the fact that he still understood what it was like to be working directly with clients and customers and therefore could relate well to his staff.

See also: Leadership, Operations Management, Top Management

Classified Board
A board structure in which part of the board is elected each year.
As a member of the 2008 classified board, Sam will serve until his tenure is done.
See also: Board of Directors, Corporate Bylaws, Governance

Clicks and Mortar
An integration of both online and traditional business; business that has both a traditional business model and an Internet model; dual channels of distribution and customer experiences, face-to-face and e-commerce; also called bricks and clicks.
The shop more than doubled its sales after moving to the clicks-and-mortar model.
See also: Bricks and Clicks, Bricks and Mortar, Business Model, E-Commerce

Client
A person who seeks the advice of a professional; the person who pays for professional service; any computer that is hooked up to a computer network.
Well-known clients are important because their very existence provides a certain comfort level to prospective customers and supplies instant credibility.
See also: Customer, Organizations, Prospect

Clip Art
Previously published graphics and art that can be imported into a presentation simply by copying and pasting; pre-made images used to illustrate any media.
The presenter used clip art to enliven the handouts and make them more interesting.
See also: Presentation Graphics

Closed Corporation
A corporation whose shares of stock are held by only a few people, usually by those who are in active management positions. Restrictions are placed on the stockholders and their right to transfer stock to others.
Most small incorporated businesses in the United States are closed corporations.
See also: Closely Held Corporation, Corporation, Stockholder or Shareholder

Closely Held Corporation

A corporation owned by a few individuals, who also own all the stock. No stock in the corporation is publicly traded. State regulations administer the establishment of corporations.

The company sold 20 percent of its shares to a group of investors, thus creating a closely held corporation instead of having to go public.

See also: Closed Corporation, Corporation, Stockholder or Shareholder

Closing

Actions and procedures required to effect the successful conclusion of a business transaction; consummation of the sale; in accounting, when the books are summarized into financial statements for a specific time frame and no further entries are allowed for this period.

The buyers had to bring the rest of the down payment and the brokers' fees to the closing of the real estate deal.

See also: Accounting, Acquisition, Assets, Period

Coaching

A method of leadership and management knowledge distribution, with the objective being deepened learning and improved performance of an individual or team.

The goal of coaching is to create a supportive environment in which to challenge and develop critical thinking skills, ideas, and behaviors.

See also: Facilitator, Mentor, Team Building

Cohort

A group, team, or band of people with some common goal or association; a group of people having approximately the same age, companions, or supporters; a group of people who share a common characteristic or experience within a defined time period.

Although cohorts can be grouped demographically, it is a mistake to assume every member of a group will react exactly the same way to the same stimulus.

See also: Period, Teams, Time Horizon

Cold Call

A seller's unscheduled approach to a prospective customer, client, or contact, either on the phone or in person. The word "cold" is used because the person receiving the call is not expecting the call.

It is often very frustrating and difficult for those making cold calls because the people who receive the calls often hang up on and reject them.

See also: Client, Customer, Prospect, Sales

Collaboration

Act of working jointly; a mutually beneficial and well-defined relationship entered into by two or more individuals, teams, or organizations to achieve common goals. The relationship includes a commitment to mutual relationships and goals; a jointly developed structure and shared responsibility; and mutual authority and accountability for success.

In order for collaboration to be successful, all parties need to be willing to perform their share of the work.

See also: Alliance, Organizations, Relationship, Teams

Collective Bargaining

The negotiations between an employer and a union representative to obtain a contract for the employees in the union.

Both sides entered into collective bargaining with realistic expectations, so the new contract was agreed upon in a matter of days.

See also: Contract, Negotiation, Union

Comfort Zone

The arena of activities that a person, team, or organization has done often enough to feel comfortable doing; a type of mental conditioning resulting in artificial mental boundaries, within which an individual or team derives a sense of security. May result when a mental concept about something is incongruent with actual reality.

The only way to break out of a comfort zone is to be exposed to other people, cultures, and experiences.

See also: Behavior, Conflict, Teams

Commercial Bank

State or nationally chartered bank that accepts demand deposits, grants business loans, and provides a variety of other financial services. Typically used by the entrepreneur as an asset lender.

Commercial banks are moving into the investment banking business both by building their own businesses and by buying investment banks.

See also: Bank, Community Bank

Commitment

The trait of sincere and steadfast fixity of purpose; an agreement or pledge to perform an act at a certain point in the future.

High-quality performers in any field or industry are usually marked by their commitment to their work.

See also: Agreement, Stakeholder

Commoditization

The rate at which products and services move from a differentiated market to a commodity market; the transformation of what is normally a noncommodity into a commodity.

These days, products commoditize so quickly that it is difficult to maintain a competitive edge in the market.

See also: Commodity, Economics

Commodity

Goods in the form of products that are bought and sold based on market supply and demand. Commodities are often traded on commodity exchanges.

Although metals and oil are traditionally considered commodities, today electronics and music are also being traded on commodity exchanges.

See also: Demand, Economics, Supply

Common Law

Rules that have been made from judicial decisions or custom without the aid of written legislature.

Under state and federal regulations, the term "offer" is broader than the common law definition.

See also: Business Literacy, Mediation

Common Stock

Shares that represent the ownership interest in a corporation; common stockholders are allowed to vote on company initiatives and are distributed dividends.

The corporation offered 100 shares of common stock as part of its signing package for new employees.

See also: Preferred Stock, Security, Stockholder or Shareholder

Communication

The flow of information and meaning between two or more people or organizations so that all concerned parties have an equal understanding.

The CEO understood communication among all of the site directors was key if the project was going to succeed.

See also: Communications Planning, Listening, Organizations

Communications Planning

The process of identifying who will need what information, when they will need it, and how the information should be formatted and disseminated. Also identifies the person responsible for providing the information.

The new product manager created an extensive communications plan for the product roll-out.

See also: Communication, Information

Community Bank

An institution that makes loans and takes deposits in one town and possibly the surrounding areas.

Small, independent companies are the major business customers for community banks.

See also: Bank, Loan

Company

A business enterprise; a firm; a legal entity that has a separate legal identity from its members and is ordinarily incorporated to undertake business.

The small mom-and-pop store eventually grew to become a globally recognized company.

See also: Incorporate, Limited Liability Company (LLC), Partnership, Sole Proprietorship

Comparative Advantage

The ability of one firm to engage in production at a lower opportunity cost than another firm.

Comparative advantage is useful in determining what should be produced and what should be acquired though trade.

See also: Competitive Landscape (Environment), Economics, Opportunity Cost, Strategic Advantage

Compensation

Wages, salary, and rewards received for employee contributions to the enterprise.

Her new position offered such a good compensation package that it was worth the long commute.

See also: Deferred Compensation, Rewards, Salary

Compensation Plan or Package

A plan or contract in which employees are paid, either directly in the form of money or by indirect such as stock options or deferred methods such as bonuses or incentives for performance.

A good compensation plan goes a long way to reducing employee turnover.

See also: Compensation, Deferred Compensation, Pay for Performance

Competencies

Knowledge, skills, and attitudes that are required for job performance.

The job was so specialized that it was difficult to find one person with all the necessary competencies.

See also: Core Competencies, Knowledge, Skill

Competition

The firms, people, and organizations that seek the same customers or position in a marketplace; a rivalry between two or more participants in a given space, market, or customer concentration.

Consumers benefit when competition among businesses keeps prices low.

See also: Competitive Position, Rivalry

Competitive Advantage

The results of strategies, actions, and decisions by management that gives a company a better chance of making money than other companies competing with it. Offering consumers greater value, either by means of lower prices or by providing greater benefits and service that justify higher prices.

The parent company was unwilling to acquire any business that did not increase its competitive advantage.

See also: Comparative Advantage, Competitive Edge, Strategy, Value Chain

Competitive Analysis

Management's study and assessment of those organizations that compete for the same customers by identifying competitors and evaluating their respective strengths and weaknesses.

Since the competitive analysis showed market saturation for the proposed project, it was voted down by the board of directors.

See also: Business Plan, Competition, Strategic Planning

Competitive Conditions

Environments, conditions, and situations that make a business able to compete with other companies in the same sector or type of business.

The technology firm underestimated the competitive conditions in the market, so it showed less of a profit than expected when the new product debuted.

See also: Competitive Landscape (Environment), Strategy

Competitive Edge

Key factors that give a company an advantage over its competitors in the marketplace; firms with sustainable, above-average earnings growth that are leaders in their industry are considered to have obtained an edge over the competition.

Often, a celebrity endorsement is enough to give one product a competitive edge over another.

See also: Competition, Competitive Advantage, Key Success Factors

Competitive Insourcing

A management process whereby internal employees engage in bidding to compete with competitive, third-party bidders for a defined scope of work.

The organization's internal employees were regularly able to compete with the bids offered by outside firms once the organization went to competitive insourcing.

See also: Efficiency, Insourcing, Management, Outsourcing

Competitive Landscape (Environment)

Understanding of where a firm resides in the business space, called a landscape or environment. The knowledge of where a firm stands or fits in relation to its competitors and the expectation that the environment (industry and global) can shift and change at any moment.

More than ever, it is important for companies to stay aware of the competitive landscape since global industries can now impact business in the United States.

See also: Competition, Economics

Competitive Position

The position of one business relative to key rivals in the same industry.

The well-known outlet store took steps to improve its performance and competitive position since exiting bankruptcy the previous year.

See also: Competitive Advantage, Strategic Intent

C

Competitive Pricing
Pricing based on evidence from the market; setting a price to be comparable to what competitors are charging.
> *When all the gas stations on the same block sell gas at the same price, it is a perfect example of competitive pricing.*

See also: Brand, Market Penetration

Competitiveness
A measure of how well a firm performs with regard to the other firms in a segment or market; how well resources are applied to a given market demand or opportunity.
> *With the outrageous success of one product, the little-known company entered into competitiveness with all the major players in the industry.*

See also: Competition, Competitive Advantage, Competitive Position

Complex Decisions
Decisions that are made in multiple levels of an organization; multiple people either deciding on or influencing the decisions.
> *Complex decisions include more considerations and more players, and those players are often located at higher levels in the organization.*

See also: Complexity, Decision Influences, Marketing, Organizations, Sales

Complexity
The quality of being intricate and compounded; managing many and often chaotic situations, organizations, and strategies.
> *The complexity of the project required a supervisor who was highly skilled in personnel management and multitasking.*

See also: Chaos, Organizations, System

Computer
A device for manipulating data according to a list of instruction that may be handheld or an entire system or network.
> *In this day and age, the ability to use a computer is a necessity for business success.*

See also: Data, Network, System

Confidentiality
Discretion in keeping secret information.
> *Maintaining confidentiality during critical business dealings is necessary in order to avoid negative consequences.*

See also: Confidentiality Agreement

Confidentiality Agreement

Contracts entered into by two or more parties in which some or all of the parties agree that certain types of information that pass from one party to the other or that are created by one of the parties will remain confidential.

Everyone in the research-and-development department had to sign confidentiality agreements or face fines and dismissal.

See also: Agreements, Confidentiality, Nondisclosure Agreements

Configuration Management

The process of ensuring that a project meets the desired outcome.

The customer approved the configuration management plan, allowing the building to proceed with construction.

See also: Change Request, Program, Program Management, Project Management

Conflict

A state of opposition between organizations, persons, ideas, or interests; an incompatibility; a disagreement or argument about important issues, strategies, or goals.

The conflict caused by the differing visions for the project caused the customer to withdraw from the firm and work with a company that could deliver what she wanted.

See also: Conflict of Interest, Conflict Resolution, Organizations

Conflict of Interest

A situation in which leadership decisions are influenced by the leader's personal interests.

When the contractor realized his company had put a bid in on a project with his wife's firm, he removed himself from consideration because of the inherent conflict of interest.

See also: Accountability, Business Ethics

Conflict Resolution

A process or means of avoiding or dealing with disputes or opposing views in organizations or between groups, teams, or individuals.

As a former mediator, she brought well-respected conflict-resolution skills to her new position.

See also: Arbitration, Communication, Conflict, Facilitator, Management, Problem Solving

Congenial

Pleasant, agreeable; able and willing to interact harmoniously with others, cooperative. A congenial person cordially welcomes new members to the organization.

Since he remembered what it was like to be new in the office, he always tried to be congenial to new hires and make them feel welcome.

See also: Cooperative, Supportive

Conglomerate

A corporation with a portfolio of business units; diverse businesses that compete in different industries, and whose growth comes largely through the acquisition of, or merger with, other firms whose products are largely unrelated to each other or to that of the parent company.

The long-term goal of the company was to slowly and quietly acquire other businesses until it had formed a conglomerate that could compete both nationally and internationally.

See also: Acquisition, Strategy

Consistent

The ability to always act/react in the same manner; steady, characterized by unvarying actions, behavior, feelings, character, beliefs, or values.

He always used the same analytical approach to decisions, making him one of the most consistent performers on the team.

See also: Reliable

Consultant

A source of knowledge and expertise to leaders and organizations; a professional who provides expertise; an advisor to top management.

The writer had a consultant to help her with the technical terms she didn't understand in the manuscript.

See also: Consulting, Professional

Consulting

A person or a firm that provides professional advisory and related client-service activities intended to add value and improve an organization's governance, leadership development, risk management, and control processes, or other services that an enterprise may need to compete.

When he first retired from the army, he worked in Hollywood doing consulting for military movies.

See also: Consultant, Leadership, Management

Consumer
Any person who uses or consumes economic goods and services.
Ad campaigns generally target a specific consumer, demographic, or age range.
See also: Business-to-Consumer (B-to-C, B2C), Consumer Credit, Consumer Demand

Consumer Credit
Credit given by a bank to a borrower for the specific purpose of purchasing a consumer good or paying for a personal expense.
As the economy weakened and fewer people were making large purchases, the consumer credit offered by lender corporations dropped dramatically.
See also: Consumer, Federal Reserve

Consumer Demand
What consumers and customers want to spend their money on; can be analyzed by businesses to predict future trends as well as identify current spending habits; how people use their limited means to make purposeful choices.
Due to the oil crisis of the 1970s, consumer demand for more fuel-efficient vehicles increased.
See also: Consumer, Demand

Consumer Goods
Items that a consumer purchases for personal or household consumption.
Sales of consumer goods tend to rise during the warmer months because people are more likely to be out shopping.
See also: Consumer, Leading Indicators

Continuous Improvement
A management process that adopts new activities and eliminates old ones found to add little or no value, with the goal of increasing effectiveness by reducing inefficiencies and waste while increasing motivation and productivity.
The firm regularly requested feedback from all of its employees in order to ensure continuous improvement throughout the organization.
See also: Kaizen, Quality, Quality Circle, Six Sigma, Statistical Control, Total Quality Management (TQM)

</>

C

Contract

A binding agreement between two or more persons or organizations that is enforceable by law; a mutually binding and documented agreement between buyer and seller covering the terms and conditions by which the work must be completed.

The contract spelled out very specifically what was expected from all parties involved.

See also: Adhesion Contract, Agreement

Control

Great skillfulness and knowledge of the business; the power to direct the management and policies of a business enterprise.

A smart manager understands what can be controlled and what can't be and doesn't try to force either one of them.

See also: Authority, Controlling, Management

Controlling

The activity of managing or exerting control over a subordinate, team, or organization; directing or determining.

The family would open the stock up to public purchase so long as they maintained the controlling interest in the firm.

See also: Control, Management, Manager

Conviction

An unshakable belief in something without need for proof or evidence.

Young business professionals often find it difficult to maintain their convictions during the early years of their careers.

See also: Beliefs, Leadership

Cooperative

The quality of being a team player; able and ready to work with others to produce a certain result; helpful and accommodating.

She received a good review for being cooperative, never complaining about assignments or workload, and being quick to offer assistance to coworkers.

See also: Collaboration, Congenial

Core Competencies

Basic skills; sources of differential advantage that are part of an organization's personality; skills, abilities, and knowledge that employees, managers, and executives must possess to achieve organizational results.

Firms with strong core competencies in those areas needed to compete will usually succeed even in difficult economic times.

See also: Competencies, Competitive Advantage, Leadership, Management, Organizations, Strategy

Corporate Bylaws

Rules concerning the internal affairs of a corporation. Filed with the secretary of state in which the corporation is incorporated.

Corporate bylaws generally can be amended by an organization's board of directors.

See also: Articles of Incorporation, Bylaws, Corporation

Corporate Objectives

What the enterprise is trying to achieve as a whole. Objectives that incorporate the entire organization or business.

The company's corporate objectives included a return on investment of at least 15 percent.

See also: Functional Objectives, Goals, Objectives

Corporation

A legal entity created under state law; form of organization that provides its owners and shareholders with certain rights and privileges, including protection from personal liability, if proper steps are followed. Most corporations are businesses for profit; they are usually organized by three or more subscribers who raise capital for the corporate activities by selling shares of stock.

The public face of a corporation is symbolized by its seal and its distinctive name.

See also: Corporate Bylaws, Incorporate, S Corporation, Secretary of State

Cost of Goods Sold (COGS)

The cost of buying raw materials and producing the goods that a company sells. Includes overhead costs and the cost of the company's labor force.

Negotiating new contracts with the suppliers improved the division's cost of goods sold.

See also: Accounting, Income Statement, Overhead

C

Cost of Living

The average price of providing the necessities for an individual; the cost of buying those goods and services that are considered to be a standard level of consumption.

She had to move to a smaller apartment because the cost of living in the city had become so high.

See also: Consumer Demand, Leading Indicators, Macroenvironmental Factors, Supply

Creative

The ability to produce something original, and often ingenious, as the result of imaginative thinking; a person with this characteristic brings imaginative, progressive thinking to new product development.

Her creative ideas brought about innovative ways of improving the efficiency and productivity of her team.

See also: Innovation, Problem Solving, Problem Taking, Value Creation

Creativity

The practice of bringing a result to existence; the art of borrowing from others in order to refine, remix, reconstitute, reassemble and evolve; out-of-the-box skills.

The team realized they needed someone who could bring a fresh perspective and creativity into the stalled project.

See also: Creative, Idea Quality, Innovating, Innovative Solutions

Credit

Money loaned. Also refers to the borrowing capacity of an individual or company; also an entry on the right-hand side of an account ledger, representing an addition to a revenue or liability account.

Few stores extend credit any longer, even to their regular customers.

See also: Accounting, Bad Credit, Credit Card, Credit Memo, Credit Rating, Credit Report, Credit Score, Liability, Loan

Credit Card

A card issued by a business that entitles the holder to purchase items on credit at participating retailers.

The average American has four different credit cards and carries a balance on all of them.

See also: Bank Card, Credit

Credit Memo

A note indicating an individual's creditworthiness or credit rating.

The credit memo on the couple assured the lending company they could indeed qualify for the mortgage.

See also: Credit Rating, Credit Score

Credit Rating

A risk assessment resulting from a formal evaluation of an individual's or company's credit history and capability of repaying debt.

The corporation's credit rating qualified them to issue AA bonds.

See also: Credit, Debt

Credit Report

A report of a company or an individual's creditworthiness; the result of an investigation into the credit background.

Many landlords require a credit report before allowing a tenant to sign a lease.

See also: Credit, Credit Rating, Lender

Credit Score

A rating for a company or individual that indicates credit risk based on historical behavior.

Lenders use credit scores to determine whether to extend credit and at what interest rate.

See also: Behavior, Credit

Creditor

A business or individual to which money is owed.

Often when a company or individual gets into enough trouble with creditors, filing bankruptcy is the only viable solution.

See also: Contract, Debtor, Loan

Crisis

A turning point or decisive moment in events; a period at which leadership is tested and organizations are stressed.

She was a strong enough CEO that what could have been a crisis for the company was forestalled and instead the episode was simply a difficulty to overcome.

See also: Decision Making, Leadership, Management, Organizations

Critical Path

The longest path through all project activities (as represented in a network diagram) that determines the duration of the project.

It was the project manager's job to ensure every step on the critical path was taken in a timely manner.

See also: Bar Chart, Gantt Chart, Work Breakdown Structure (WBS)

Critical Path Method (CPM)

A technique used to determine the duration of a project by looking at the sequence of activities and their flexibility in scheduling.

The developer used the CPM to explain to the team exactly what steps needed to happen concurrently in order to make the deadline.

See also: Critical Path, Gantt Chart, Program Evaluation and Review Techniques (PERT), Project Management

Critical Success Factors (CSFs)

Areas of activity in which favorable results are absolutely necessary to reach goals; key areas where things must go right for the business to flourish; elements that are necessary for an organization or project to achieve its mission.

The CSFs must be made clear to all involved because if any of them slips through the cracks, the project could fail.

See also: Key Success Factors, Strategic Objectives

Cross-Functional Team

A group of employees from various functional areas of an organization, assembled as a team and empowered to solve problems that cross organizational boundaries; people working toward a common goal and made of people with different functional expertise.

In order to bring the company into the global market, a cross-functional team was created to address the needs of every department.

See also: Organizations, Team Building, Teams, Teamwork

Culture

Attitudes, beliefs, character, and sets of important assumptions that members of an organization share.

The culture of the firm needed to change if it was going to attract women and minorities onto its staff.

See also: Beliefs, Organizations, Stakeholders

Current Assets

Assets that are easily convertible to cash; cash or property that can be converted to cash in a short period of time, usually accounts receivable, inventory, and short-term notes receivable. Reported on the balance sheet.

Short-term investments and accounts receivable are current assets that should result in cash within the next year.

See also: Accounts Receivable, Assets, Cash

Current Liabilities

A debt that is payable within one year or within the normal operating cycle of a company; usually accounts payable, accrued expenses payable, and short-term notes payable.

The holiday season brought in enough profits to ensure the small shop could pay off its current liabilities, regardless of how strong sales were the rest of the year.

See also: Accounts Payable, Accrued Expenses, Liability, Loan

Current Ratio

The ratio of a company's current assets to its current liabilities. The current ratio provides a speedy indication of a company's ability to meet short-term debt obligations. A current ratio of less than 1-to-1 typically indicates a poor credit risk. A current ratio of greater than 2-to-1 typically indicates a good credit risk.

Banks examine a company's current ratio closely before issuing a loan.

See also: Current Liabilities, Ratio Analysis

Customer

An individual, business, or other organization that purchases or makes the decision to buy a product or service from a business entity. It is the customer who determines what a business is.

Most companies need to continue to increase their customer base in order to stay in business.

See also: Client, Customer Loyalty

Customer Loyalty

A result of high customer satisfaction for a product or service; the quality of customers returning to the product or business time and time again; company resources are employed so as to increase the loyalty of customers and other stakeholders in the expectation that corporate objectives will be met or surpassed.

Car manufacturers depend on customer loyalty as much as new innovations to stay competitive.

See also: Customer Satisfaction, Stakeholders

Customer Relationship Management (CRM)

The strategy of designing an enterprise around customers and their wants and needs; the process of developing and maintaining a relationship with customers through interactive technology, loyalty-reward programs, and direct-mail messages, in order to encourage repeat business.

CRM is based on the concept that good customer relationships are at the heart of business success.

See also: Customer Service, Marketing, World Wide Web (WWW)

Customer Retention

Keeping customers who have done business with the firm through programs to provide service, customer relationship management, and sales techniques. Long-term customers tend to be less inclined to switch and also tend to be less price sensitive. This can result in stable unit sales volume and increases in dollar-sales volume.

Customer retention is vital to the success of a business because it is generally more expensive to acquire a new customer than to keep an existing one.

See also: Customer Relationship Management (CRM), Customer Service, Marketing, Sales

Customer Satisfaction

Making customers happy; making customers pleased with their purchases and aware of a product's real-world benefits.

Changes were made to the car as a direct result of the customer satisfaction surveys.

See also: Benchmark, Competitiveness, Customer Loyalty, Customer Retention

Customer Service

An organization's ability to supply its customers' wants and needs and to increase the customer's convenience and satisfactions.

Good customer service can make up for a problem or difficulty with a sale.

See also: Customer Relationship Management (CRM)

Cutting Edge

Being out front of the competition; the position of greatest advancement; forefront; the leading position in any market, technology, movement, or field.

The firm was constantly hiring the brightest minds in the industry in order to stay on the cutting edge of technology.

See also: Creativity, Innovation

D

Data

A set of facts, figures, statistics, details, particulars, specifics; information, intelligence, material, input; informal info before it is processed into information.

The data collected for a project must be accurate or else every decision made thereafter will be faulty.

See also: Data Communication, Data Management, Data Mining, Data Processing, Data Warehouse

Data Communication

Electronic transmission of information that has been encoded digitally.

The small business leased its data communication network rather than purchasing it.

See also: Database, Internet Protocol (IP), Local Area Network (LAN), Network, Wide Area Network (WAN)

Data Management

The development and execution of architectures, policies, practices, and procedures that properly manage the full data lifecycle needs of an enterprise; maintaining and managing data as an organizational asset.

Many companies are using data management and other technology to offset reduction in staff.

See also: Computer, Data, Data Mining, Database, Information

Data Mining

The ability to scan a data pool for common factors, organizing the data to reveal a pattern; information extraction activity whose goal is to discover hidden facts contained in databases.

The interns used data mining to find the patterns in recent sales of similar products for the presentation to the board.

See also: Competitive Intelligence, Data Warehouse, Market Research

Data Processing

Manipulation of data by a computer in order to retrieve, transform, or classify information; involves recording, classifying, sorting, summarizing, calculating, disseminating, and storing data.

Accurate data processing is essential in record keeping and maintaining databases.

See also: Data, Data Communications, Information

Data Warehouse

A system or database that contains large volumes of historical business data. A resource for data mining.

The auditors required information from deep within the data warehouse, proving that appropriate records had been kept.

See also: Data Mining, Market Research

Database

A collection of data arranged for ease and speed of search and retrieval; an organized collection of data stored in a systematic way.

Every night, the administrative assistant backed up the database to ensure the information would be safe and secure.

See also: Data, Computers, Information, Software Applications, Systems

Deadlines

The date or time at which something needs to be completed or a payment made.

The team put in long hours and worked weekends and was able to meet the scheduled deadline in spite of not getting the project until very late.

See also: Milestone, Project

Deal Flow

The steady flow of transaction opportunities into a firm; the rate at which new projects and proposals are created in a service business.

As the firm's reputation grew, so did the deal flow coming into the business.

See also: Opportunities, Projects

Debenture

A written promise by a corporation to repay money that has been borrowed. This certificate or voucher is usually referred to as an unsecured corporate bond or promissory note.

The new parent company promised to pay off all the outstanding debentures as part of the buyout agreement.

See also: Debt, Interest

Debit

An entry in the left side of an account ledger representing an increase in an asset or expense account.

Companies keep a customer's voided check on file, which allows them to debit the customer's bank account for the amount owed.

See also: Accounting, Assets

Debt

Something owed or an obligation, such as money or services, to another person.

In a barter situation, professionals will often pay off debts by offering services rather than cash or monies.

See also: Debt Capital, Debt Service, Liability

Debt Capital

Funds or assets acquired by borrowing.

The debt capital was enough to keep the small business afloat until it was financially stable.

See also: Debt, Debt Service, Loan

Debt Service

The money needed to pay the amount due on a loan.

Obtaining the loan at a reasonable interest rate allowed the restaurant to grow and still cover the debt service.

See also: Debt, Interest, Loan

Debtor

A company or individual who owes a debt.

Most companies are willing to work with debtors in order to avoid turning off services or taking legal action.

See also: Debt, Debt Service, Loan

Decentralized

Power and authority pushed downward in an organization, enabling employees to have a greater voice in how things are done.

Once the chain went national, it moved to a decentralized sales force in order to ensure they were closer to their customers.

See also: Bottom-Up, Decision Making, Organizations, Top-Down

Decision Influences

The quantity of individuals or organizations required to fund or maintain funding for a project or contract.

During budget reductions, the number of decision influences increased.

See also: Complex Decisions, Decision Maker, Decision Making

D

Decision Maker

The person within a company who ultimately decides which products or services to buy; a role that a potential customer assumes when making decisions about products or services that are wanted or needed.

As the decision maker for the team, she had to juggle the problems of making decisions quickly and at the same time, finding as much information on the subject as possible.

See also: Buyer, Client, Customer

Decision Making

The cognitive process leading to the selection of a course of action among alternatives; selecting a course of action for an enterprise, team, or project; selecting between alternatives.

The new director insisted that all decision making be based on the new values declared in the rewritten mission statement.

See also: Group Processes, Groupthink, Problem Solving

Decision Support Systems (DSS)

Systems that improve the effectiveness of managerial decisions; software that speeds access and simplifies data analysis, queries, and so on within a database management system.

The five most appealing scenarios were run through the computer's decision support system to see if one or two really stood out as particularly desirable or undesirable.

See also: Decision Making, Management, Management Information Systems (MIS)

Decisive

Able to make firm decisions and make distinct, clear-cut determinations; to decide without hesitation.

The board was decisive in its decision to sell the company rather than face bankruptcy.

See also: Decision Making, Leadership

Dedicated

Devoted to a principle, belief, or purpose; characterized by belief in the goals/objectives/purposes of the enterprise.

He is dedicated to building a strong distribution system for the business.

See also: Goals, Leadership, Principled

Deduction

An item that can be subtracted from income to determine a company's taxable income.

The temp agency took new training programs as deductions since they were necessary business expenses.

See also: Income, Taxes

Deep Pockets

Having more financial resources to invest in ventures and projects than other contenders, groups or organizations. Also the most likely to be sued for damages in the case of a business failure.

Investors with deep pockets are more likely to be able to acquire businesses simply because they can make higher bids for the purchase.

See also: Investment, Venture Capital

Default

A failure to pay a debt, to make scheduled payments, or to meet any term of a credit contract; nonpayment of principal and/or interest.

Lenders will take legal action if a loan is in default for too long, so it is best to deal with them rather than try to avoid the situation.

See also: Credit, Debt, Loan, Payments

Deferred

An accounting situation in which a payment is due but is not given credit as a payment until a later date.

The option of deferred taxes often makes certain investments more appealing than others.

See also: Accounting, Credit, Payments

Deferred Compensation

An incentive program in which an amount is earned but is withheld until a later date. Examples of deferred compensation include pensions, retirement plans, and stock options. The primary benefit of most deferred compensation is the deferral of tax.

Stock options have been a preferred method of deferred compensation in many industries for decades.

See also: Pension, Stock Option

D

Defined Benefit Pension
A type of pension plan in which the sponsor distributes to the qualified employees a guaranteed amount of retirement income.

The company's older employees were especially grateful for the defined benefit pension since Social Security was not as reliable as it had been in the past.

See also: Benefits, Deferred Compensation, Pension, Pension Fund, Pension Plan

Delegation
Getting things done through other people; the process of empowering others in the down line of an organization to act with authority; organizational or team contribution to achieving a goal by giving and receiving assignments toward a common end.

The project manager delegated the scheduled tasks to her team.

See also: Assign, Authority, Teams

Delinquency
A past-due credit account or debt payment.

Paying bills on time prevents accounts from entering into delinquency.

See also: Credit, Debt, Payment

Delivery
A process for transporting and distributing something; the receipt of goods from the seller to the desired location of the buyer.

Vendors must offer reliable and timely delivery if they are going to succeed in business.

See also: Distribution, Distributor, Logistics

Demand
The amount of a particular economic good or service that people are both willing and able to buy or that a group of consumers will want to purchase at a given price.

As the holidays approach, the demand for the most popular new toy increases markedly.

See also: Consumers, Economics, Supply

Demand Note
A note that is payable immediately when the holder decides to present it.

After the small business was late paying off its loan, the bank issued a demand note for the monies to be repaid in full within thirty days.

See also: Liability, Payable

Demographics

The science of grouping human populations statistically by such character-istics as age, sex, family size, income, and occupation. Demographics is a shorthand term for "population characteristics."

The Country-Western style chain decided not to expand into New England based on the demographics of the area.

See also: Market Research

Demotion

The reduction in a worker's status to a lower grade, rank, salary, or title.

The team leader was grateful for the demotion instead of being fired when the team missed the deadline for the project.

See also: Change, Promotion

Deposit

Cash and checks given to a bank to maintain a credit balance until the funds are withdrawn and converted to cash.

Every morning, the clerk made the deposit from the sales generated the day before.

See also: Bank, Cash, Credit

Depreciation

An accounting procedure for the allocation of the cost of a long-term asset over its useful life; average or expected view of the decline in value of an asset. Depreciation reduces taxable income without reducing cash.

The depreciation of the equipment on paper did not affect its actual function-ing, thus making it a worthwhile purchase for the small company.

See also: Accelerated Depreciation, Amortization, Book Value, Devaluation, Straight-Line Depreciation

Differentiation

A shift in the source of competitive advantage through the process of mak-ing one thing or process different from another. Providing an offering, pro-cess, business model, or set of offerings that the customer believes deliver superior performance per unit of cost.

Whenever a product is marketed, the company searches for the differentiation that will make this product more appealing than similar ones already avail-able to the public.

See also: Strategy

Digital Manufacturing

The ability to describe every aspect of the design-to-manufacture process digitally—using digital design, analysis, simulation, and manufacturing tools.

The technicians presented the entire project to the investors using digital manufacturing in order to prove the process could be cost effective.

See also: Lean Manufacturing, Manufacturing, Productivity, Reengineering

Diligent

The characteristic of working with intense concentration. A person with this characteristic perseveres, even after repeated frustration, applies him or herself thoroughly and persistently, works steadfastly toward goals, and shows strong commitment to undertakings.

The accountant's diligent attention to the books prevented anyone from being able to embezzle from the company.

See also: Consistent, Serious

Direct Mail

Selling directly to a prospective customer via the U.S. Postal Service or a private delivery company.

The nonprofit organization ran a direct-mail campaign every six months hoping to bring in donations.

See also: Direct Marketing, E-Tailer, End User, Retailer

Direct Marketing

Marketing directly to the end user with marketing campaigns including e-mail, direct mail, telemarketing, and other targeted messages.

Direct marketing is a proven and effective tool in creating new customers and finding new business.

See also: 1-to-1 Marketing, Customer Relationship Management (CRM), Direct Mail

Directing

Leading individuals or groups by providing direct instructions; giving directions clearly and unequivocally, such that people know exactly what to do and when.

The young supervisor was surprisingly effective in part because he never needed the express support of his own supervisors in managing and directing his department.

See also: Leadership, Management, Management Style

Direction

The process of managing a person, team, or organization; setting and holding a course. Concentration of attention or energy on a goal or strategy.

The CEO had asked the facilitator to move the group in the direction of scrapping the project if at all possible.

See also: Controlling, Goal, Management, Organization, Strategy, Teams

Dirty Data

A problem found in databases when some data is missing or incorrectly entered, thus causing information culled from the database to be false or inaccurate.

The quality-control staff had a hard time finding the cause of the dirty data, but they finally discovered the data entry glitch and were able to get the project back on schedule.

See also: Customer Relationship Management (CRM), Data, Database

Disbursement

The act of paying out funds to satisfy a financial obligation.

The lawsuit was settled for a one-time cash disbursement instead of going to court, which could have ended up costing the company more.

See also: Accounts Payable, Payable, Payments

Disclosure

The public release of information; act of releasing all relevant information pertaining to a company that may influence an investment decision.

The firm had a policy of full disclosure of the financial records in order to avoid even a whisper of scandal.

See also: Investment

Discount Rate

A rate of return used to convert a future monetary sum into present value. Also the interest rate the Federal Reserve charges on loans to its member banks.

The CFO took the discount rate into consideration before recommending to the board that the company diversify.

See also: Internal Rate of Return (IRR), Net Present Value (NPV), Time Value of Money

Discounted Cash Flow

What someone is willing to pay today in order to receive an anticipated cash flow in future years; a method to value a project or an entire company. Businesses use discounted cash flow to judge whether an investment project is worthwhile. Money received in the future is worth less than money earned today. To compensate, the future incomes are discounted to their present-day value.

The discounted cash flow showed the deal to be far less lucrative than it appeared on paper.

See also: Cash Flow, Cost of Capital, Net Present Value (NPV), Opportunity Cost, Risk, Time Value of Money

Discretion

The managerial trait of judging wisely and objectively; power of making free choices unconstrained by others.

The team leader was able to use her own discretion in handling matters, so she rarely had to present her supervisor with problems.

See also: Leadership

Discrimination

The act of displaying prejudice against another individual due to race, religion, age, or some other reason not related to job performance.

A charge of discrimination can be damning for a company.

See also: At-Will Employment, Business Ethics

Distribution

The process of getting a finished product from the manufacturer to the customer.

The best way for a company to ensure freshness of perishable goods is to ensure the distribution process is as streamlined as possible.

See also: Distribution Channel, Logistics, Marketing, Retailer, Sales, Wholesaling

Distribution Channel

The path to the end user of a product or service. A given distribution channel may include marketing and merchandising methods, responsible organizations, as well as the tools and techniques for creating and maintaining that channel. Distribution channel examples include distributors, wholesalers, retailers, e-commerce, direct marketing, and self-service outlets.

Few customers realize the distribution channel required to get a product from the factory to the store.

See also: Distribution, Marketing, Sales, Wholesale Sales Method

Distribution Cost

The cost incurred in marketing and shipping a product from the manufacturer to the end consumer.

Retail prices need to cover distribution costs in order for manufacturers to make a profit.

See also: Distribution, Distribution Channel, Marketing

Distributor

A person or company that markets or sells merchandise, especially a wholesaler; someone who buys large quantities of goods and resells to merchants rather than to the ultimate customers.

The distributor expects to receive a significant price discount for providing the goods.

See also: Distribution, Sales

Diversification

A growth strategy in which a business markets new products in new markets; risk-reduction method that involves spreading assets among many different investments. Diversification may occur internally within the team or organization or, more often, through strategic alliances, acquisitions, or joint ventures.

The technology firm realized that diversification was the key to staying in business.

See also: Acquisition, Strategy

Divest

To dispose of an interest or transfer a title.

The company decided to divest its interests in the small country when the human rights violations were reported and confirmed.

See also: Asset Redeployment, Boston Consulting Group Box (BCG Box), Strategy

Dog

Underperforming venture, product, or firm that is characterized by losing market share and/or declining growth. Usually an unattractive opportunity in a poorly performing market sector with cash flows that are break-even or negative.

As long as the company was breaking even, the old man refused to sell his shares even though it was a dog.

See also: Boston Consulting Group Box (BCG Box), Cash Cow, Strategy

D

Doing Business As (DBA)

A situation in which a business owner operates a company under a different name than the one under which it is incorporated. The owner typically must file a fictitious-name statement or similar document with the appropriate county or state agency.

Instead of launching a media frenzy, the movie star opted to stay anonymous and use a DBA when she opened her own boutique.

See also: Company

Domain Name

Location on the Internet that serves as the Internet address and is unique for every Web site.

Creating an easily accessible and somewhat obvious domain name is important to the success of online businesses.

See also: Internet, Web Page, World Wide Web (WWW)

Downsizing

Across-the-board cutting of staff for cost reduction; a reduction in the number of an organization's personnel; a permanent elimination of positions as a cost-cutting measure (or for other reasons.)

The downsizing that occurred throughout corporate America in the 70's and early 80's effectively put an end to employees being loyal to one company for an entire career.

See also: Attrition, Layoff, Organizations, Outplacement, Rightsizing

Downtime

A period in which a machine, department, or factory is idle during normal working hours.

The techs tried to keep machine downtime to a minimum because of the cost to the plant when production was halted.

See also: Operations, Productivity

Due Diligence

The assessment and research performed in advance of an investment or opportunity; the process of assessing risk; an examination of operations and management and the verification of material facts.

Although the investment looked good on paper, due diligence showed it to be risky at best.

See also: Investment, Mergers and Acquisitions (M&A), Takeover

E

E-Commerce

Buying and selling (engaging in commerce) over the Internet; business transactions facilitated by electronic technology, including private telephone and cable lines, Internet Web sites and e-mail, and corporate intranets.

The advent of e-commerce has allowed people to open shops and reach customers when it would have been financially impossible in the past.

See also: Business-to-Business (B-to-B or B2B), Business-to-Consumer (B-to-C or B2C), E-Mail, Internet, World Wide Web (WWW)

E-Mail

Short for electronic mail. The process of one user employing a computer to send a text message to an electronic mailbox to be retrieved and viewed by another user.

E-mail is not only a way to stay in touch with friends but is also an excellent way of communicating with colleagues, receive feedback from investors, and stay in touch with a board of directors.

See also: Communication, Computers, Information Technology (IT), Internet, Software

E-Mail Marketing

The promotion of products or services via e-mail. When used correctly, and ethically, e-mail marketing is one of the most effective forms of online advertising.

Many stores attach coupons to enhance the effectiveness of their e-mail marketing campaigns.

See also: Direct Marketing, E-Commerce, E-Mail, Marketing

E-Tailer

A retail e-commerce business; a store that uses the Internet as a means of interacting with customers.

E-tailers must compete with physical stores on every level in order to be successful instead of expecting the convenience of shopping from home to override poor quality, a lack of customer service, or limited inventories.

See also: E-Commerce, Internet, Retailer

Earnest Money

Partial payment in advance, showing the serious intent of a buyer.

The buyers put down $5,000 earnest money to prove they really wanted the house.

See also: Front Money

Earning Per Share (EPS)

A profitability ratio of net income available to common shareholders to the number of common shares outstanding; a traditional method used for determining corporate value and a widely used measure of a company's stock performance.

The broker compared the value of several different companies using the EPS before recommending a trade to any of his clients.

See also: Financial Ratios, Stockholder or Shareholder, Valuation

Earning Per Share (EPS) equals the amount of net income per share of stock. Wall Street likes to use **EPS** as means of measuring a stock's performance, like so: the **EPS** for Q3 was $0.25, which was a 15 percent increase year over year.

Earnings Before Interest, Taxes, Depreciation, and Amortization (EBITDA)

A measure of cash profitability, often of an operating unit.

Even though the business was small, its EBITDA was high enough the bank was comfortable giving out the large loan.

See also: Depreciation, Interest, Leveraged Buyout (LBO), Taxes

Earnings Before Interest, Taxes, Depreciation, and Amortization (EBITDA) is the measure of cash generation of a firm. Many investors use this number especially when dealing with granting loans to a company. Debt owners use **EBITDA** as a means of seeing how much "cash generation" a business can cover your interest expenses.

Economics

The branch of social science that deals with the production and distribution and consumption of goods and services and their management.

A parent company that owns a subsidiary with superb long-term economics is not likely to sell that entity, regardless of price.

See also: Microeconomics

Effectiveness

A means of measuring productivity; power to be effective; resources spent in achieving the desired effect.

The young man's interruptions and posturing did not hinder the effectiveness of the training because the facilitator maintained control of the group.

See also: Management Effectiveness

Efficiency

The ratio of the output to the input of any system, organization, or enterprise; the characteristic of avoiding waste; improved or better use of resources.

The plant's level of efficiency rose after the old, outdated equipment was replaced.

See also: Resource Allocation, System

Elasticity

The flexibility or resilience of the economy to change; a measure of the responsiveness of one variable to changes in another.

The elasticity of a product can vary according to the amount of close substitutes, its relative cost, and the amount of time that has elapsed since the change occurred.

See also: Demand, Economics, Price, Substitute, Supply

Elevator Pitch

A brief overview of an idea for a product, service, or project. Describes the twenty to sixty seconds an entrepreneur has to interest a venture capitalist in his or her business idea—about the same amount of time as the entrepreneur would have if he or she ran into the venture capitalist in an elevator and had his or her (unwilling) attention for the ride.

An elevator pitch is a good way for anyone from a sales professional to a politician to get a point across to many people quickly.

See also: Communication, Entrepreneur, Executive Summary, Presentations, Venture Capital

Emergence

The act of coming (or going) out; process of complex organizational pattern formation from more basic constituent parts or behaviors; becoming visible.

The emergence of online services, from banking to laundry pick-up and delivery, has made it easier than ever to have very little face-to-face customer interaction.

See also: Behavior, Complexity, Organization

Employ

To engage an individual or a company to perform a job in exchange for compensation.

The busy woman chose to employ a housekeeping service rather than spend her little free time cleaning her house.

See also: Compensation, Employee

Employee

An individual who works for an employer in exchange for a wage or salary.

The entrepreneurs were thrilled when their company grew enough to justify hiring another employee.

See also: At-Will Employment, Employ, Salary

Empowerment

A management style that gives employees the power to make decisions about the work to be done as well as how the work is to be done.

The new CEO believed that the empowerment of all the employees, even those at the lowest levels of the organization, would eventually create loyalty and a better-running company.

See also: Decision Making, Organizational Development, Responsibility, Team Building

End User

The ultimate customer, client, person, or group that will use a product or service.

The tech firm kept the end user in mind when developing the new software so that it would be complex enough to handle the programs but simple enough that even novices could be comfortable using it.

See also: Client, Customer, Value Chain

Energetic

Managers, executives, and employees who work actively toward a desired goal/objective; characterized by vigorous activity, and never seeming to tire.

Our regional manger is energetic, making repeated sales calls to prospective clients without tiring.

See also: Diligent, Goals

Engineering

The planning, designing, construction, and management of a product or project.

The engineering team developed a specification for the new product.

See also: Management, Planning, Product, Project

Enterprise Resource Planning (ERP)

A system that consolidates an enterprise's planning, manufacturing, sales, and marketing efforts into one management system that allows executives to plan, organize, and control key sectors of activity, such as purchasing, inventory, suppliers, customer service, and order tracking.

If designed well, ERP software should be capable of running an enterprise without much input.

See also: Management, Manufacturing, Marketing, Planning, Resource Allocation, Sales

Entrepreneur

Someone who is willing to take risks and solve problems and is eager to create a new venture in order to present a concept to the marketplace in the pursuit of profit.

The entrepreneur chose to open her business in her old neighborhood, hoping to bring foot traffic into the area and rebuild its reputation.

See also: Growth, Innovation, Problem Solving, Risk

Entrepreneurs see change as the norm and as healthy. The **entrepreneur** always searches for change, responds to it, and exploits it as an opportunity.

Entrepreneurial Chaos

Organized chaos; an idea-rich environment with change being the only constant; entrepreneurial activity while highlighting elements of turbulence, change, and unpredictability.

During the first six months, the feeling of entrepreneurial chaos made the new firm an exciting, if somewhat challenging, place to work.

See also: Competitive Advantage, Complexity, Creativity, Entrepreneur

Entrepreneurial Organization

A culture that promotes growth, risk-taking, opportunity-seeking, innovation, and adapting to change; a small-company feel and climate; competitive teams leveraging intellectual capital.

Even after becoming very successful, the partners refused to let the firm get so big that it lost the feel of an entrepreneurial organization.

See also: Entrepreneur, Entrepreneurial Chaos, Entrepreneurship, Innovation, Leverage, Opportunities, Risk

Entrepreneurship

A management practice of innovation and risk taking; a process through which individuals and groups pursue opportunity, leverage resources, and initiate change to create value.

His encouragement of entrepreneurship allowed even lower-level employees to present new ideas and suggestions.

See also: Entrepreneur, Entrepreneurial Chaos, Innovation, Leverage, Opportunities, Risk

Entry Barriers

A number of different factors that restrict the ability of new competitors to enter and begin operating in a given industry; obstacles on the way of potential new entrant to enter the market and compete with the incumbents.

The entry barriers finally proved too overwhelming for the small company to overcome, so they had to close their doors.

See also: Exit Barriers, Industry, Obstacles, Rivalry Among Industry Competitors, Strategy

Entry barriers are those things that make it difficult for a new company to compete against companies already established in the field. **Entry barriers** benefit existing companies already operating in an industry because they protect an established company's revenues and profits from being whittled away by new competitors.

Ephemeralization

Doing more and more with less and less. The theory that gradually smaller and smaller amounts of materials and effort will accomplish more and more useful functions. Finding ways to take existing resources and use them in different ways. Being creative with resources; looking at things from a different perspective.

The cutbacks led to the ephemeralization of the department that, eventually, caused the staff to become more creative and actually more successful.

See also: Integration, Management, Resources, Synergy

Equity

Ownership interest in a business; the total or intrinsic value of an asset. Total assets minus total liabilities equals equity or net worth.

Many don't understand that owning stock in a business is similar to having equity in their own homes.

See also: Assets, Balance Sheet, Brand Equity, Equity Financing, Ownership, Return on Equity (ROE), Stock

Equity Financing

The means of financing a business; funds invested in a business by its owner(s); capital or operating expenses in exchange for capital stock, stock purchase warrants, and/or options in the business financed, without any guaranteed return, but with the opportunity to share in the company's profits.

Many investors are willing to use equity financing to invest in high-risk ventures because they expect to make larger amounts of money once the business goes public.

See also: Capital, Equity, Financing, Investment, Operating Expense, Options, Stock, Venture Capital, Warrants

Excellence

Superior performance in leadership, teams, organizations, or individuals; possessing good qualities in high degree; the state or quality of excelling.

The hotel chain strived for excellence in all aspects, from grounds keeping to concierge-level services.

See also: Goals, Organizations, Success, Values

Exception

A deliberate act of omission; making an exclusion.

The billing department made no exceptions when it came to getting accounts paid on time or owing late fees.

See also: Exception Management, Exclusion, Omission

Exception Management

The process of systematically eliminating or minimizing the negative impact of exceptions; a means of extending the span of control and simplifying the management of an enterprise.

Retail stores implement exception management by selling seconds at outlet and discount stores.

See also: Exception, Management, Management Philosophy

E

Exchange Rate
The rate at which one unit of currency can be converted into that of another currency.
The exchange rate was so good that the tourists got luxury items for half of what they would have paid at home.
See also: Foreign Exchange Rate

Exclusion
Something that is specifically outside a contract or agreement; a deliberate act of omission.
The exclusions in the shipping contract included antiques and items valued at more than $5,000.
See also: Agreements, Contract, Exception, Inclusion

Execution
The process of performing, doing something successfully; act of accomplishing some aim or executing some order; effective implementation.
The manager had specific requirements regarding the end results of the project but left the actual execution of the process to her team.
See also: Accomplishment, Implementation, Management Effectiveness, Performance

Executive
A person who holds a position of authority, is responsible for strategy, and leads an organization, business, or corporation.
The board of directors authorized a financial package aimed at keeping the executives with the company.
See also: Authority, Leadership, Organizations, Strategy

Executive Summary
A concise presentation of a plan, project, or report's major findings, conclusions, and recommendations. As the initial face presented to a potential investor, it is critically important that it create the right first impression.
Several drafts of the executive summary were written before one was finally good enough to present to prospective investors.
See also: Abstract, Business Plans, Proposals

Exit Barriers

Obstacles that impede an organization from leaving its sector, tier, or industry; obstacles to market players who realize that they will not turn a profit and would like to quit the market.

The failing company was stuck because of the exit barrier created by having no other alternative product to produce.

See also: Entry Barriers, Industry, Obstacles, Rivalry Among Industry Competitors, Strategy

Exit Interview

An interview conducted at the end of an activity; a discussion that occurs at the end of an employee's term of employment; the completion of a project; the termination of a relationship.

The man struggled with how honest to be in his exit interview because he needed his supervisor's recommendation for any future jobs.

See also: Group Interview, Interview, Project, Relationship, Research Interview

Expenses

An outgoing payment made by a business or individual that is reported on the firm's income statement.

The accountant assured the CEO that the expenses paid to the consultant were well within the yearly budget.

See also: Income Statement, Payments

Experienced

Having knowledge or skill as a result of education, training, and experience; expert in a particular function or role.

The entrepreneurs brought in an experienced public relations firm to help launch the new enterprise.

See also: Knowledge, Skill

Expert System

A tool businesses use to make more effective decisions and to solve problems quickly using a computer or network to aid in the decision process.

The "help" section of a computer's taskbar is the most widely known and accessed expert system.

See also: Artificial Intelligence, Knowledge Management, Problem Solving

Extranet

E

An extension of a company's intranet to information users from outside the enterprise.

All the vendors had access to the company's extranet system in order to get the information they needed without having to speak to someone on the phone.

See also: Communication, Data Management, Information, Internet, Intranet, Network

F

Face Value

The amount printed on a bond or other debt instrument, which it repays at maturity and on which the borrower computes interest.

The face value of the loan was insignificant, but the interest made it a much larger amount to repay.

See also: Bond, Debt, Interest

Facilitating

A means for developing leadership and an organization; the process of making easy or easier the tasks of a team; designing and running a successful meeting, retreat, panel, or seminar session.

Her calm demeanor when she was facilitating meetings made her ideal whenever the topic was a particularly emotional one.

See also: Facilitator, Meetings

Facilitator

A process guide, someone who makes a process easier or more convenient. Someone who helps to manage a process of information exchange, who uses some level of intuitive or explicit knowledge of group processes to formulate and deliver some form of formal or informal process intervention.

The board meetings required a strong facilitator or else they would become free-for-alls and nothing would be accomplished.

See also: Meeting, Organizational Development

Farsighted

The ability to look to the future. A person with this characteristic is able to anticipate future events or developments and their likely implications and strives to anticipate new opportunities.

Entrepreneurs need to be patient and farsighted because most new ventures take several years to make a profit and become truly successful.

See also: Insight, Vision

Feasibility Study

A study undertaken to determine whether a project is viable; research to determine the economic feasibility of a proposed business venture.

Although the director liked the concept, she ordered a feasibility study before giving final approval.

See also: Business Plan, Project, Venture

Fee

A charge for professional services rendered; price paid as remuneration for services, especially the honorarium paid to a member of a learned profession.

Many people believe that a high fee guarantees high-quality service.

See also: Cancellation Fee, Retainer, Wage

Feedback

Positive or negative information provided to an organization or individual that is used to shape behaviors and that should closely follow an action for maximum result.

The program director was not good at taking negative feedback from her staff, so eventually they stopped speaking to her and started speaking about her behind her back.

See also: 360-Degree Feedback, Behavior, Coaching, Organizations, Systems

Feet on the Street

The concept that states if a company has more people in its sales force, it will sell more product. A company may increase, decrease, or maintain its feet on the street.

The small business decided to decrease its feet on the street in order to put more money into ad campaigns.

See also: Prospecting, Sales, Sales Representative

Finance Charge

Total interest in dollars and cents paid to obtain credit.

The doctor's policy was to add a finance charge on accounts that were more than forty-five days late.

See also: Credit, Interest

Financial Literacy

Ability to use financial language; working knowledge of financial concepts and the tools for effective financial decision making. An individual's ability to solve or dissolve problems, at levels of proficiency necessary to function on the job, in an organization, or in the marketplace.

The man realized that he needed someone with a high level of financial literacy to help him with the money he inherited from his parents.

See also: Business Literacy, Credit

Financial Ratios

Financial comparisons that can be used to establish baseline figures; comparisons can be year to year, company to company or company to industry.

The management team dictated which financial ratios were to be studied in order to measure the company's success.

See also: Metrics, Ratio Analysis

Financial Statement or Report

A statement of a firm's financial condition, including financial flows and levels; accounting of activities. Usually includes a balance sheet, income (profit and loss) statement, and cash flow statement.

The stockholders were pleased with the financial statements released after the merger.

See also: Balance Sheet, Cash Flow, Income Statement, Profit and Loss (P&L) Statement

Financing

Providing or arranging for the capital needed for a business to prosper, either by way of equity infusion or loans (debt). The science of the management of money and other assets.

The first thing the woman did in order to open her salon was find the financing to fund the operation.

See also: Bank, Credit, Investment

Firewall

A means of protecting an enterprise information system from being compromised; computer software or device that connects a local network to the Internet and for security reasons allows only certain kinds of messages in and out.

The small business installed a firewall when they opened their e-commerce store.

See also: Computer, Internet, Local Area Network (LAN), Network, Security, Wide Area Network (WAN)

First In First Out (FIFO)

An accounting method of valuing the cost of goods sold, stocks, or other items that uses the cost of the oldest item in inventory first. Therefore, the ending inventory consists of items that were the last ones manufactured or purchased.

The FIFO method is useful to track different shipments of similar products.

See also: Accounting, Cost of Goods Sold (COGS), Inventories, Last In First Out (LIFO)

First-Round Financing

The first infusion of capital in a new venture after the initial seed money has been exhausted.

Since the company delivered such a strong, initial presentation, they received first-round financing with very little effort.

See also: Seed Capital, Seed Stage, Venture Capital

Fiscal

Anything relating to a firm's finance or finances.

Since it never had enough money, the nonprofit worked very hard at being fiscally responsible.

See also: Assets, Debt, Financial Statement, Fiscal Year, Liabilities, Retained Earnings

Fiscal Year

A company or corporation's accounting period that consists of twelve consecutive months.

All the grant money had to be spent by the end of the fiscal year in order for the nonprofit to qualify for the grant again.

See also: Accounting, Fiscal, Period

Fixed Asset

Property with relatively long life, such as land, buildings, and equipment. Reported on the firm's balance sheet.

The board of directors hoped to find a way out of the financial trouble without selling any of the company's fixed assets.

See also: Asset, Balance Sheet, Capital Expenses (CapEx)

Fixed Capital

Money invested in fixed assets.

Property values were increasing quickly enough that the firm felt comfortable putting most of its fixed capital into real estate.

See also: Fixed Asset, Investment

Fixed Cost

A cost of doing business, such as rent and utilities, that remains generally the same regardless of the amount of sales of goods or services. These costs remains constant regardless of a change in production.

Even during the recession, her shop was always able to pay for the fixed costs, so she never worried about going under.

See also: Accounting, Income Statement

Flexible

Capable of changing with the times; low resistance to change; able and willing to adapt to new or different circumstances, situations, or ideas.

Only the staff that was flexible enough to incorporate the changes stayed with the company after the merger.

See also: Change, Change Management

Flipchart

A method of communicating information to a group, team, or organization using a large pad of paper supported on an easel; consistently one of the most popular forms of visual aids for business facilitators.

The trainer depended on his flipcharts as much as his PowerPoint slides during his presentations.

See also: Communication, Organizations, Teams, Visual Aid

Float

The time frame between when a check is deposited in the payee's bank and when that check is cleared by the payer's bank (sometimes refers to the amount of money in the process of being collected, represented by the number of checks yet to be cleared); or the portion of a company's stock that is still available for public trading; or the amount of time that the early start of an activity can be delayed without affecting the completion date of the project (also known as slack time).

He knew the check would clear because he had cash to deposit during the float.

or

Within hours after the stock went on sale, the float was reduced dramatically.

or

The technicians hoped the manufacturing line would be back up and running during the float time because otherwise millions of dollars could be lost.

See also: Bank, Information, Project Management

F

Floppy Disk
A thin, soft, flexible, and plastic-like diskette that magnetically stores data.
The floppy disk was the main method of backing up personal computers in the 1980s.
See also: Memory, System

Flowchart
A graphical representation for the definition, analysis, or solution of a problem; a graphical representation for a process; diagram showing the steps in a process or system from beginning to end.
The project manager used a flowchart in her presentation that showed the steps in the process from beginning to end.
See also: Problem Solving, Project Management, System

Fluff
Information in a presentation used to entertain or motivate, as opposed to educational or business information.
A good presentation has enough fluff to keep the audience's attention but not so much that the speaker loses its interest.
See also: Meetings, Oral Presentations, Visual Aid

Focus
The quality of selecting the right things to pay attention to; avoiding distractions; avoiding being spread too thin and being overwhelmed. A person with this characteristic runs a tight ship, with business practices enhancing the one special value that he or she can provide better than anyone else.
Rather than branching out, the company decided to focus on improving its current products.
See also: Leadership, Management

Focus Group
A method of learning about customer preferences by using a group of people who are asked to provide qualitative information regarding products, concepts, ideas, packaging, promotional campaigns, and other market-testing needs.
Focus groups are an important tool for acquiring feedback regarding new products.
See also: Group Processes

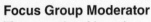

Focus Group Moderator

The person hired by a client to lead a focus group.

The focus group moderator had his work cut out for him because most people deferred to the senior member present instead of offering their own ideas.

See also: Facilitator, Focus Group, Panels

Follow-Up

A management activity that continues something that has already begun or that repeats something that has already been done.

The program director requested a follow-up report on the results of the action plan meeting from all of the supervisors.

See also: Diligent, Effectiveness

Followership

A characteristic of people in support positions that best suit the leadership characteristics to implement change.

The staff's followership was a testament to how much they trusted the management team during the transition.

See also: Change, Change Management, Leadership

Forecast

An estimate or prediction of future expectation by using the best available information. Used by businesses to establish goals, plan investments, and manage the enterprise based on a forecast of revenue and expenses.

Investors often make decisions based on the forecast of certain stocks, corporations, or industries.

See also: Budget, Sales Forecast, Uncertainty

Forecasting

The art and science of developing a forecast; use of tools such as models, statistics, tends, and historical data to extrapolate into the future.

Even the best, most educated forecasting is just guesswork, and investors are wise to remember that fact.

See also: Forecast, Planning

Forfeiture

The loss of cash or property, resulting from a breach of a legal obligation.

The landlord held the firm's assets in forfeiture when the rent wasn't paid in full after six months.

See also: Contract, Obligation

Franchise

A form of contract between two parties, usually a manufacturer and a retailer. Relationship and license in which the franchisor provides a licensed privilege to the franchise to do business and offers assistance in organizing, training, merchandising, marketing, and managing in return for a consideration.

When consumers boycott certain companies, the individual franchise owners feel the pinch long before the parent company.

See also: Contract, Franchising

Franchise Agreement

A written contract or agreement between franchisor and franchisee that covers such things as length, termination, obligations, territory, and royalties. Sets forth the expectations and requirements of the franchisor.

The franchise agreement must be followed closely in order to maintain the right to use the parent company's name and reputation.

See also: Agreement, Contract, Franchise, Royalties

Franchising

A method of doing business within a given industry through a distribution system. A parent company is linked to independent companies that buy a right to own and operate the franchise along the lines of the parent company's comprehensive marketing program.

Franchising has become a popular way for retirees to invest their nest eggs and stay involved in business.

See also: Distribution, Franchise, Franchise Agreement, Marketing

Free Cash Flow

Company's net cash flow from operating activities minus capital expenditures for property, plant, and equipment; cash that's leftover after everything—bills from suppliers, salaries, expenses, new equipment to expand the business—has been paid out. The hard cash that is available to pay the company's various claim holders, in particular the shareholders.

The CFO kept a close eye on the company's free cash flow to ensure its continuing viability.

See also: Cash Flow, Liquid

Free Enterprise

The freedom with which a firm or an individual is able to organize and operate in a competitive environment without excessive government intervention.

The U.S. economy is based on the concepts of capitalism and free enterprise.

See also: Economics

Free Trade
The movement of goods between countries in the absence of harsh restrictions placed upon this exchange.

Many people believe free trade between developed and developing countries will strengthen the economies of all the countries involved.

See also: Globalization

Freeze
To maintain prices or wages at a fixed level.

During a state of emergency, officials will often freeze prices to prevent people from taking advantage of the situation.

See also: Price, Wage

Friendly Takeover
The acquisition of one company by another at the invitation of the first company.

Small companies often prefer friendly takeovers because they allow the company to have some input into the decision-making process.

See also: Acquisition, Merger, Strategy

Front Money
Early-stage investment money provided for initial efforts to launch an enterprise; same as seed money.

The young politician received most of the front money she needed for the campaign from her friends and family.

See also: Earnest Money, Seed Capital, Seed Stage

Functional Objectives
The intended achievements of functional organizations, aims that are specific, measurable, achievable, relevant, and time bound.

The company's functional objectives were included in all the paperwork sent out to potential investors.

See also: Objectives, SMART Criteria

Functional Organization
An organizational structure that groups staff hierarchically by area of specialty.

The electronics manufacturing firm set up a functional organization to manage the business, with a sales, marketing, operations, and finance vice president leading each department.

See also: Organizations, Staff

Furlough

A leave of absence from duty or work, usually requested by the employee.

The program director granted the woman a three-month furlough when her father became ill so she could make the necessary arrangements for his care.

See also: Vacation

Future Emphasis

A practice organizations utilize that is a strategic view of the future. The things that are dominant in a long-range plan or business forecast.

The retreat shifted the management thinking from the past to a future emphasis.

See also: Business Plan, Forecast, Organizations

Future Value

The value at some point in the future of a present amount of money; what money is worth at a specified time in the future assuming a certain interest rate. May be an asset or cash.

The contracts were signed based on the estimated future value of the company's overall worth.

See also: Discount Rate, Time Value of Money

Fuzzy Logic

A tool for making decisions and selecting options that improves decision quality when the available data is imprecise or scarce.

Fuzzy logic is controversial in some circles, despite wide acceptance and a broad track record of successful applications.

See also: Artificial Intelligence, Decision Making, Expert System, Uncertainty

G

Gantt Chart

A graphical representation of a project schedule, with the focus primarily on schedule management.

Each supervisor's role was delineated clearly on the Gantt chart so every department could stay on track.

See also: Bar Chart, Business Plan, Work Breakdown Structure (WBS)

Gatekeeping

The process of regulating the flow of information; controlling which information will go forward, and which will be filtered out.

The CEO's assistant couldn't type or create a database but she excelled at diplomatic gatekeeping, so he kept her on his staff.

See also: Barrier, Communication, Information, Obstacles

Gateway

A Web page designed to attract visitors and search engines to a particular Web site; a combination of hardware and software that provides merchants with the ability to perform real-time credit card authorizations from a Web site over the Internet. The link between a merchant and the bank.

A typical gateway page is small, simple, and very user-friendly since its primary purpose isn't to sell itself but to lead clients to other, larger sites.

See also: Authorization, E-Commerce, Internet, Link, Merchant Account, Search Engine, Shopping Carts, Web Page, Webmaster, World Wide Web (WWW)

General and Administrative (G&A) Expenses

Expenses to manage the enterprise that are incurred in providing the product or service but that do not include the actual/direct costs of the product or service. G&A expenses include officer salaries, legal and professional fees, utilities, insurance, depreciation of office building and equipment, and stationery supplies. Reported on the income statement.

The shop owners kept G&A expenses low by often working from home.

See also: Income Statement, Overhead, Pro Forma

General Ledger

A general ledger is an accounting term for the primary record that, when used in conjunction with subsidiary ledgers, contains all of the balance sheet and income statement accounts.

The auditor's main job was to find any discrepancies in the general ledger and investigate them.

See also: Accounting, Balance Sheet, Income Statement

General Manager

An individual responsible for overseeing the day-to-day operations of a business unit, division, or branch office of a company.

The mechanic hired a trustworthy general manager so he could focus on his customers and their cars.

See also: Management

Generally Accepted Accounting Principles (GAAP)

The standards used by firms and their audit partners for keeping and reporting accounting data in the United States; also referred to as U.S. GAAP.

The company uses the accelerated depreciation method, which is compliant under U.S. GAAP.

See also: Bottom Line, Free Cash Flow, Income Tax

Generation X

Consumers born between 1965 and 1976. Key characteristics include quest for emotional security, independence, informality, and entrepreneurial nature.

Although Generation X was originally seen as selfish and self-centered, their entrepreneurial spirit has effected incredible growth in many industries.

See also: Cohort, Market Research, Marketing

Generation Y

Consumer born between 1983 and 2007. Key characteristics include quest for physical security and safety, patriotism, heightened fears, acceptance of change, and technical savvy.

Generation Y's attitudes may always be defined by coming of age in a post–9/11 world.

See also: Cohort, Market Research, Marketing

Globalization

A widening of corporate operations across borders to produce and sell goods and services in more markets; the ability to extend a company's market worldwide with the use of technology and newly established distribution channels; the trend for people, firms, and governments around the world to become increasingly dependent on and integrated with each other.

Some people are concerned that continued globalization will cause businesses in the United States to become too dependent on other countries for goods and raw materials.

See also: Free Trade

Goals

The object of a team, organization or person's ambition or effort; an aim or desired result. specific targets which are intended to be reached at a given point in time. A goal is thus an operational transformation of one or more objectives.

The company's goals were to change the industry, not just be another player in it.

See also: Objectives

Going Public

Executing an initial public offering to allow the average investor the opportunity to acquire and own a portion of the corporation; selling shares to the public for the first time.

The board of directors finally decided two years after the founder's death that going public was acceptable.

See also: Initial Public Offering (IPO), Liquid

Golden Parachute

Benefits provided to executives as an incentive to remain with the organization and to discourage an unfriendly takeover.

The company was known for the golden parachute it offered all members of its executive-level staff.

See also: Benefits, Compensation, Deferred Compensation

Goodwill

Intangible assets that represents the difference between the market value of a firm and the market value of its net tangible assets.

After the scandal, the large corporation was willing to pay the extra money to acquire the goodwill owning the smaller business would bring to the table.

See also: Balance Sheet, Financial Statement or Reports, Intangible Assets

Goodwill is the missing piece of a company's value. When a firm (acquirer) buys another firm (target), the balance sheet of the target must reflect the fair market value of the firm's assets and liabilities. This is done because assets and liabilities are recorded at cost, so this will cause significant under valuations over time. The remaining piece that is not covered by fair market value is **goodwill.**

Governance

The combination of processes and structures implemented by the management, project or board in order to inform, direct, manage and monitor the activities of the organization toward the achievement of its objectives, including the structure of the roles, responsibilities and relationships between the leadership and the organization's long-term operational decision makers.

The board realized a more responsive system of governance would be required after the reorganization in order to avoid previous pitfalls.

See also: Organizational Effectiveness, Value Based Management

Grant

Financial support made available for specific projects or nonprofit organizations that have a favorable interest rate or are not expected to be repaid.

The organization had to eliminate three positions when it did not get grants to pay the salaries.

See also: Nonprofit Corporation (Not-for-profit), Organizations

Gross Margin

A measure of how profitable a business is before the infrastructure costs are considered. The higher the gross margin, generally, the healthier the business. Net sales minus cost of goods sold; computed by dividing gross profits (sales minus cost of goods sold) for a period by the revenues for the same period.

During the regional expansion, the CFO reassured the board that, in spite of their initial concerns, the gross margin was not dropping.

See also: Cost of Goods Sold (COGS), Income Statement, Revenue

Gross Profit

Also called gross margin, the difference between what a company spent in production of all its products and what it made in sales. Subtracting all money spent (cost of goods sold) from money made (net sales) results in gross profit on sales. Gross profit is an amount that appears on the income statement.

The small business had high enough gross profits that it was able to spend more on development, thus making it a player on the market far sooner than anyone expected.

See also: Cost of Goods Sold (COGS), Income Statement, Profit

Gross Sales

Sales or revenue in a given period before any expenses are deducted.

The gross sales for the quarter were strong enough that the manager took her team out for lunch to celebrate.

See also: Income Statement, Revenue, Sales

Group Discussion

A forum where ideas, concepts, and issues are shared and debated in a group setting and where participants interact as a team.

Hoping to create a team feeling rather than simply issuing a directive, the department head asked the people involved in the project to have a group discussion about what changes needed to be made.

See also: Focus Group, Group Interview, Netiquette, Panels, Portal, Team Building

Group Interview

A qualitative research technique involving a discussion among eight to ten respondents, led by a facilitator or moderator.

The teenagers were brought in for a group interview when the community center decided to expand its services to high school students.

See also: Facilitator, Focus Group, Group Discussion, Interview, Moderator, Panels

Group Processes

A means of improving the effectiveness or efficiency of a group, team, or organization.

The group leader drew up a draft agenda and designed the group process to attain the necessary results.

See also: Change Management, Culture, Decision Making, Facilitator, Focus Group, Organizational Development, Team Building, Teams

Groupthink

The problem that arises when maintaining peace within a group becomes more important than looking at an issue in an objective, fact-based way. May occur if a group is tightly knit and highly loyal to one another, if everyone within the group shares similar ideas, or if there is a strong group leader who makes his/her opinions known. May be countered by asking someone ahead of time to voice unpopular ideas, asking the leader to refrain from expressing his or her opinion, or providing an opportunity for truly anonymous feedback/suggestions.

The subcommittee had worked together for so long it was falling victim to groupthink without even realizing it until the new boss pointed it out.

See also: Decision Making, Leadership, Organizations

Growth

The increase and change in an enterprise or organization over time; a process of becoming larger.

While expansion is usually a good thing, uncontrolled growth can cause financial damage and even cause companies to fail.

See also: Change, Emergence, Growth Rate

Growth Capital

Cash invested, needed, spent or sought to fund the growth/expansion stage of business development.

The airline waited to expand until it had the growth capital necessary to do so without risking overextending itself.

See also: Capital, Mezzanine Financing, Private Equity

Growth Industries

Segments and industries predicted to show abnormally rapid growth in the future.

Job hunters and investors are always on the lookout for the next growth industry.

See also: Growth, Growth Rate, Industry

G

Growth Potential
The difference between a venture's present sales volume and its sales potential.
The growth potential of the new product was huge assuming it could be marketed properly.
See also: 10X, Growth, Sales, Venture, Venture Capital

Growth Rate
The rate increase and change in a product, service, business, or project over a period of time; usually expressed in a percentage.
The prediction was for the product's growth rate to settle in at about 5 percent after the initial sales rush.
See also: Average Annual Growth Rate, Growth

Growth Stage
Characterized by rising sales, substantial profits, increased demand, increased competition, improved cash flow, improved liquidity, and high leverage.
The successful start-up entered the growth stage sooner than even the most optimistic investors had expected.
See also: Growth, Leverage, Life Cycle, Liquid

Guerrilla Marketing
A method of growing a business in which profits rise as the marketing investment diminishes. Guerilla marketing uses nontraditional, economical methods to accomplish the marketing tasks for a business and creative methods and means of creating and keeping customers. The primary investments of marketing should be time, energy, and imagination.
Although the directors were initially surprised by the guerilla marketing tactics suggested by the advertising department, they came to see the brilliance in the new ideas.
See also: Campaign

Guidelines
Principles for management; detailed plan or explanation aimed at providing guidance in setting standards or determining a course of action; a rule or principle that provides guidance to appropriate behavior.
The training manual spelled out the guidelines for most foreseeable situations that might arise.
See also: Behavior

Guild

An organization of members with similar interests, skills, culture, and pursuits.

Many artists join guilds for the social aspects as well as the professional benefits.

See also: Culture, Organizations, Skill

H

Handout

A takeaway from a business presentation or meeting; promotional or educational material given to each audience member; relevant information that someone needs to learn or take action.

The handouts were effective because they were brightly colored, well designed, and interesting for the participants to read.

See also: Presentation Slides, Visual Aid

Hard Assets

Assets that can be converted to cash; balance sheet asset with liquidating value, such as equipment and machinery.

Many start-up businesses will use hard assets to secure larger loans that allow them to continue to grow.

See also: Asset-Based Financing, Balance Sheet, Capital Expenses, Liquid

Hard Sell

Sales techniques that put strong pressure on the buyer and require the seller to be very aggressive.

He much preferred his new company's laidback approach, which allowed the product to speak for itself, over the hard sell that had been required at his last job.

See also: Sales

Harvest

To liquidate accumulated assets and equity of a venture, thus converting a profitable investment in cash to realize a profit from the investment.

The CEO was hesitant to enter into any collaboration without having a harvest strategy in place ahead of time.

See also: Boston Consulting Group Box (BCG Box), Strategy

Helpful

Willing to assist; provides support to others.

The secretary had a reputation for being helpful in completing projects from different departments so long as her own work was done.

See also: Collaborate, Cooperative, Supportive

Hierarchy

The organization of people at different ranks; a system of ranking and organizing things or people in which each element of the system (except for the top element) is subordinate to a single other element.

The company's hierarchy was so strict and so well defined that resentment from the lower levels was inevitable.

See also: Organizations, Structure

High Technology

A market segment characterized by highly skilled employees, many of whom are scientists and engineers, as well as venture capital investments, a fast rate of growth, a high rate of research and development expenditures to sales, high risk/high return, and a worldwide market. High technology is both very advanced and continuously changing at a much faster rate of progress than other industries.

Most industries see greater growth and faster expansion due to high technology, thus making accurate long-range planning more difficult and more necessary at the same time.

See also: Innovation, Technology, Technology Transfer

Home-Based Business

An entrepreneurial business operated from the proprietor's own home. Often referred to as small office/home office or SOHO business.

She chose to sell beauty products so she could have a home-based business while her children were young.

See also: Entrepreneur

Host

A networked computer that provides information or services to other computers.

The IT department had one employee whose sole job it was to maintain and update the host so it wouldn't crash and cause the entire network to fail.

See also: Client, Computers, Local Area Network (LAN), Network, Server

Human Capital

The knowledge, skills, and competencies of people in an organization.

The business brought human capital as well as strong stocks to any merger thus making it a valuable acquisition.

See also: Core Competencies, Knowledge Management, Skill

Human Resources

The activities associated with recruiting, development (education), retention and compensation of employees and managers.

Every year, human resource managers from major corporations all over the world came to the university for recruitment.

See also: Compensation, Employee, Human Capital, Management

Hype

The generating of media excitement about a product or service.

Although they didn't ignore the hype, they refused to get cocky about the success of the upcoming release.

See also: Media, Product, Public Relations

Hyperinflation

A period of overwhelming inflation in which currency becomes virtually worthless.

The Great Depression of the 1930s is the most notable example of hyperinflation to ever occur in the United States.

See also: Economics, Inflation

Hyperlink

A marked or otherwise emphasized phrase on a Web site that leads to another document when clicked.

Users who click on a banner typically follow a hyperlink to the advertiser's Web site.

See also: Banner Ad, Hypertext, Internet, Web Page, World Wide Web (WWW)

Hypertext

Used in Web documents, a method of preparing and publishing text in which readers can choose their own paths through the material by clicking on certain words or phrases.

The Internet is a vast collection of information in hypertext format on home pages.

See also: Internet, Link, Network, Web Page, World Wide Web (WWW)

I

Icon

A small image on a computer screen that represents an application, file, or folder.

His desktop was covered with icons showing pictures and graphics.

See also: Application, Computer, Image, Network

Idea Quality
The measurement that looks at how likely an idea is to receive funding. A concept with high idea quality is more likely to receive funding than one with a low idea quality.

The young entrepreneurs knew they had to convince the potential backers of their product's high idea quality or they would never get money.

See also: Entrepreneur, Innovation

Ideal Capacity
The largest possible production volume for a factory operating at maximum efficiency.

Many seasonal manufacturing businesses operate at ideal capacity during peak time of the year.

See also: Capacity, Efficiency, Manufacturing, Operations, Production

Idiosyncratic
Peculiar to the individual; a structural or behavioral characteristic peculiar to an individual or group.

A wise businessperson remembers that even the ideas of the best consultant are idiosyncratic and must be weighed carefully.

See also: Behavior, Organizations, Teams

Idle Capacity
Unused capacity in conjunction with a lack of raw materials or skilled labor.

When the winery is waiting for the grapes to be picked, there is idle capacity in the bottling lines.

See also: Capacity, Production, Raw Materials

Idle Time
Time when an employee, team, or organization is unable to perform its tasks and activities due to a breakdown in the machinery required for production.

The bottling line was down due to a broken part so the crew spent idle time waiting for it to be repaired.

See also: Idle Capacity, Production, Teams, Time Management

Illiquid
Being short of cash when debts are due.

The accountant warned the board that if changes were not made soon, the company would be illiquid within six months.

See also: Cash, Debt, Liquid

Immediate-Response Advertising

An advertising gimmick to cause the potential consumer to buy a particular product within a relatively short time.

Short-term specials and same day offers are often effective forms of immediate-response advertising.

See also: Advertising, Marketing

Implementation

An act of accomplishing some aim or executing some order; implementing; providing a practical means of achieving a plan, task, or goal.

Even though the implementation of the changes would take several months, the expected increase in productivity would make the delay worthwhile.

See also: Management, Organizations, Planning, Resource Allocation, Strategy Implementation

Import

To receive goods or services from one country into another.

Many islands must import the goods needed for daily life, which can make them more expensive than local products.

See also: Importer

Importer

A firm or individual who buys goods from foreign markets.

As a third-generation importer of luxury goods, he could spot a quality item over a cheap imitation quickly.

See also: Buyer, Import

Inclusion

Something that is specifically included in a contract or agreement; a deliberate act of submission.

The attorney questioned the woman's inclusion of her pets in the will.

See also: Agreements, Contract, Exclusion

Income

The amount of money received.

The toy manufacturer nearly doubled its annual income when the latest product became the "must-have" toy for the holidays.

See also: Revenue, Sales, Wages

Income Statement

Record of a company's earnings or losses for a given period of time, typically a year, a quarter, or month. Shows all income generated by the business, such as earned (revenues), and all money spent (expenses) during this period. Also accounts for the effects of some basic accounting principles, such as depreciation. The income statement is important for management because it's the basic measuring stick (metric) of profitability. The income statement provides the stakeholders with much insight to the company's activities, such as where the company spends much of its income, to facilitate comparing a company's performance with previous years and if the business is profitable. The income statement should help investors and creditors evaluate the past performance of an enterprise, predict future performance, and assess the risk of achieving future cash flows.

Research and development (R&D) is an expense reported on the income statement, reflecting the company's effort to discover and invest in new technologies.

See also: Accounting, Financial Statement or Reports, Metrics, Profit, Profit and Loss (P&L) Statement

Income Tax

Tax paid by businesses as a portion of net income.

Many businesses usually pay their income tax quarterly rather than having to pay it all on April 15.

See also: Income Statement, Taxes

Incompetence

Lack of ability or qualifications.

Although the applicant interviewed well, her poor performance revealed her incompetence within a few weeks of being hired.

See also: Competencies, Peter Principle

Incorporate

To form a corporation according to the laws governing incorporation of a business, which are different in the different states.

Once her small housecleaning business grew to a statewide agency, she decided it was time to incorporate.

See also: C Corporation, Corporation, S Corporation

Incubator

A means of accelerating the successful development of entrepreneurial companies; a setting for getting a start-up company off the ground by providing some of the essential services that are common to young organizations.

Today, incubators often prefer cash to equity as payment for their services.

See also: Entrepreneur, Innovation, Organizations, Start-Up

Indecision

Inability or unwillingness to make a decision; doubt when it comes to choosing between options or alternatives; managerial procrastination.

The CEO's indecision concerning major issues caused turmoil in his organization and with the shareholders.

See also: Decision Making, Indecisiveness, Leadership

Indecisiveness

Doubt concerning two or more possible alternatives or courses of action; a lack of firmness of character or purpose.

The entrepreneurs' indecisiveness around the venture capital funding caused the investors to withdraw their offer.

See also: Decision Making, Indecision

Independent

The ability to work autonomously; able to act on one's own, without direction, help, or approval from others; a person with this characteristic makes effective decisions without seeking the opinions of others.

The CEO needed an assistant who was independent, efficient, and driven.

See also: Decision Making

Industry

A group of firms that market products that are close substitutes for each other; basic category of business activity; any grouping of businesses that share a common method of generating profits.

The computer industry was one of the fastest growing in the 1990s.

See also: Business Activity, Substitute

Inflation

A general increase in prices, resulting in a decline in the purchasing power of money. Its opposite is deflation, a process of generally declining prices.

Although inflation tends to cause wages to rise, they rarely match the corresponding hike in prices.

See also: Economics, Price

Informal Organization

The way things get done in organizations; relationships, networks, and culture that facilitate work and creativity.

As much gets accomplished behind the scenes in the informal organizations within a company as gets accomplished within the confines of the set job duties.

See also: Adhocracy, Hierarchy, Program, Project, Structure, Teams

Information

Knowledge, instruction, communication, representation, and mental stimulus acquired through study or experience or instruction; a message received and understood; intelligence developed from data.

The Internet has made more information available to more people than has ever been accessible before.

See also: Artificial Intelligence, Communication, Data, Information Technology (IT)

Information Literacy

Knowledge or competency in information and systems; the ability to recognize when information is needed and to locate, evaluate, and use effectively the needed information. A person with this skill recognizes that accurate and complete information is the basis for intelligent decision making.

Information literacy is no longer about being able to read, write, and perform mathematical functions but now includes computer skills, political awareness, and a basic understanding of the world.

See also: Business Literacy, Financial Literacy, Information, Information Technology (IT)

Information Technology (IT)

The methods and systems to process data and information; the physical elements of computing, including servers, networks, and desktop computing that enable digital information to be created, stored, used, and shared.

In an increasingly computerized world, businesses depend more and more on strong IT departments to stay up to date.

See also: Data Management, Information, Internet, Technology, World Wide Web (WWW)

Infrastructure

The basic structure or features of a system or organization; management, planning, finance, and accounting procedures of a firm.

In spite of the major changes caused by the merger, the basic infrastructure of the company remained the same.

See also: Management, Network, Organization, Planning, Structure

Inhibit

To use power or authority to limit the range or extent of a thing or action; to restrict.

Laws have been enacted to inhibit certain business practices, such as cornering markets and creating monopolies.

See also: Pent-Up Demand, Suppress

Initial Investment

The money needed to get a venture off the ground.

The business took longer to get off the ground because the entrepreneurs had underestimated the initial investment needed to get everything running.

See also: Investment, Seed Capital, Venture Capital

Initial Markup

The original price increase added to a product before any markdowns.

The e-commerce company's initial markup kept their prices below those in the retail stores.

See also: Markdown, Markup, Price

Initial Operations Stage

A chaotic stage of development that an enterprise may experience, characterized by inefficient work and production processes, fluctuating production and overhead costs, and employee turnover.

Once they got past the initial operations stage, the next challenge was to develop a distribution system and get their products into the marketplace.

See also: Entrepreneurial Chaos, Life Cycle, Overhead, Production, Turnover

Initial Public Offering (IPO)

First sale of stock (equity) to the public; the action of making an IPO is referred to as "going public." An IPO is a method of raising capital for growth, expansion, and to change the debt-to-equity ratio.

Investors were very excited about the IPO of the new technology firm that showed such promise.

See also: Equity, Growth Capital

Innovating

Creating and experimenting with ideas; the process of making innovations; dealing with uncertainty and taking risks.

By constantly innovating and investing in R&D, the tech firm managed to stay at the front of the industry for years.

See also: Gatekeeping, Innovation, Trailblazer

Innovation

A new method, idea, or product as the result of a process for facilitating and exploiting change; a conceptual and perceptual means of creating new knowledge that makes old knowledge obsolete by introducing something novel or unique to the marketplace.

Most simple products that we now take for granted were once great innovations that captured the imagination of the country.

See also: Change, Innovating, Product Development

Attitudes toward **innovation** will be determined by the business philosophy of an organization. In a more forward-thinking company, innovation is often encouraged and supported. In a team environment, another's **innovation** is not resented but celebrated, so long as it is of benefit to the team and the company as a whole.

Innovative Solutions

A means of delivering innovation to the end user. This job belongs to concept development teams that attempt to develop an innovative match between emerging technology and a new requirement.

When faced with challenges, the most successful businesses are able to find innovative solutions in order to create results anyway.

See also: End User, Innovation, Solutions, Teams, Technology

Inputs

Information that is required for a process to begin.

Although the manufacturer had received most of the inputs necessary, it was still missing some vital parts, so production could not begin on time.

See also: Data, Information, Process, System

Insight

An intuitive grasp of the inner nature of things; "getting it." The clear (and often sudden) understanding of a complex situation.

The information provided by the anonymous responses gave the management team better insight into the feeling of the overall staff.

See also: Complexity, Intuition, Situation, Understanding

Insolvency
The inability of a business to meet financial obligations; having insufficient assets to pay legal debts. Often results in bankruptcy.

After several projects went to competitors, the construction company saw that it was facing insolvency if it didn't get a large contract soon.

See also: Bankruptcy, Debt, Liability

Insourcing
Transferring an outsourced function to an internal department of a company to be managed entirely by employees; retaining service "inside" the organization.

Insourcing the company cafeteria may create a small team of "den mothers" who are on hand to bake cookies, encourage exercise, or offer a shoulder to cry on during stormy office romances.

See also: Organizations, Outsourcing

Intangible Assets
A nonphysical claim to future value or benefits; amortized on a straight-line basis over their estimated lives. Notable intangible assets are goodwill and copyrights.

While the book value of the small company was low, the intangible assets that came with the merger could not be overstated.

See also: Assets, Franchise, Goodwill, Human Resources, Innovation, Intellectual Property, Patents

Intangible Rewards
Recognition in a form other than monetary that an employee receives from the employer, such as being praised for a job well done or given in-house recognition for outstanding performance.

The company provided a picnic for the team at the completion of the project as an intangible reward.

See also: Behavior, Compensation, Payment, Recognition, Rewards, Team

Integration
The process of combining separately created organizations and altering them so that they can interact and be more productive than the independent elements; developing synergy and value by developing strategic interdependence among functions.

The integration of the two staffs after the merger was one of the most difficult challenges faced by the director.

See also: Synergy, Vertical Integration

Integrity

The quality of knowing what is important and living and taking action accordingly. Derives from honesty and consistent uprightness of character.

The dean of the business school challenged her graduates to not only find success but to find it while maintaining their integrity.

See also: Authority, Character, Values

Intellectual Capital

Ideas that foster competitiveness; the knowledge assets that a company owns; the ideas and knowledge possessed by key employees that make a company competitive.

The intellectual capital within the company was worth far more than the hard assets because they only hired the brightest minds available.

See also: Entrepreneurial Organization, Human Capital, Intangible Assets, Intellectual Property

Intellectual Property

A work or invention that is the result of creativity, such as a manuscript or a design, to which one has rights and for which one may apply for a patent, copyright, trademark, or other protection; intangible property usually developed from the knowledge, ideas, and talent of individuals.

The Internet and the ability to share information easily have created an interesting legal tangle around intellectual property rights and how to enforce them.

See also: Copyright, Patent

Intelligent

The ability to bring uncommon reasoning to decision making; a person with this characteristic thinks out precisely what steps are necessary to reach a goal or an objective before taking any action.

The investor's intelligent reading of the marketplace allowed him to sell several stocks before the industry crashed.

See also: Decision Making

Interest

The cost of using money, usually obtained through a loan or other form of borrowing. A cost for credit that is determined by rate and time of use.

The couple made an extra payment on their mortgage every month in order to pay off the principle and reduce their interest.

See also: Annual Percentage Rate (APR), Credit, Debt Service, Interest Rate, Loan, Time Value of Money

Interest Rate

The percentage charged or applied to a loan or credit for the use of funds.

Many credit card companies offer very low interest rates for the first year in order to attract customers.

See also: Annual Percentage Rate (APR), Bond Yields, Interest

Interested

The quality of finding one's work highly stimulating; attention or concern aroused and held.

The interested customer service manager seeks out knowledgeable employees or industry experts to help solve problems hindering her progress.

See also: Motivated

Interface

The area of overlap where two groups or organizations affect each other or have links with each other.

Due to the interface between the sales and marketing departments, the two staffs worked very closely with one another.

See also: Organizations, Project Management, Teams

Internal Rate of Return (IRR)

The growth rate of a firm's invested capital over a time period relative to the amount invested. Used by managers to compare investment projects. IRR, which compares the profit to the amount invested, is expressed as a percent gain or loss for easy comparison with other percent changes for the same time period. The IRR calculation is based on continuous compounding.

The IRR indicated that continued investment in the project was worthwhile.

See also: Discounted Cash Flow, Rate of Return, Time Value of Money

Internet

A network of online sites that connects business, consumers, and governments. A global method of reaching customers, suppliers, and users.

The Internet has changed the face of business in only a few decades.

See also: Intranet, Net, Network, Web Page, World Wide Web (WWW)

Internet Protocol (IP)

A format for packaging and sharing data on the Internet; provides the service of communicable unique global addressing amongst computers.

Brian had to know her IP address to know if her computer was connected to the Internet.

See also: Data Communication, Internet

Interview
A question-and-answer session between employer and applicant in order to assess the applicant's qualifications for a position.

The interview was geared more toward learning the applicant's management style than about the specific position.

See also: Exit Interview, Group Interview, Research Interview

Intranet
A private corporate network built with Internet-based protocols, World Wide Web browser technology, and software applications used by business as infrastructure.

Only company employees had access to the intranet and then only from their office computers.

See also: Internet, Net, Network, Web Page, World Wide Web (WWW)

Intrinsic Value
The actual value of a company, as opposed to its market price or book value. Includes other variables such as brand name, trademarks, and copyrights that are often difficult to calculate and sometimes not accurately reflected in the market price or valuation. May also be a value of an enterprise or an asset based on an underlying perception of what the stockholders believe it is worth.

The intrinsic value of the company, considering its reputation and long history of success, was far greater than its book value.

See also: Discounted Cash Flow, Time Value of Money

Intuition
Instinctive knowing; gut feel; hunch.

The investor relied as much on her intuition as the hard data presented her when deciding which companies to back.

See also: Innovating, Observant, Vision

Inventories
Products, work-in-process, and raw materials used by a business for resale. Reported on the firm's balance sheet as current assets.

Most stores increase their inventories during the months leading up to the holiday shopping season.

See also: Raw Materials

Inventory Control

A management process of balancing incoming and outgoing stock, products, and deliverable items to assure that adequate supplies are on hand with which to do business.

Without decent inventory control, a shop will end up with too many of one item and not enough of another.

See also: Inventories, Management, Stock

Inventory Turnover (Turnaround)

A measure of the rate in which inventory is moved; called "turn" for short, it represents the number of times a firm sells and replaces (turns over) its merchandise in inventory in one year; a ratio for evaluating sales effectiveness. For a given accounting period, divide total revenue for the product by the average retail value of the product inventory.

At Christmas, the toy stores' inventory turnaround on the latest hot game was so high that few parents could find it on the shelves.

See also: Financial Ratios, Inventories, Inventory Control

Investing

Using capital to grow more capital; laying out money or capital in an enterprise with the expectation of profit; may also be used in the sense of using time or resources wisely.

Investing for the long-term can be an effective and lucrative way to make money for retirement.

See also: Capital, Economics, Investment, Profit

Investment

The application of human and fiscal capital to develop a successful strategy; putting resources to work to create wealth and value; the outlay of money for the purpose of making more money for either income or profit or both.

The artist's investment of time, money, and energy finally paid off when he was able to open a second gallery outside of the city.

See also: Bonds, Capital Investments, Human Capital, Infrastructure, Security, Stock

Investor

A business or person who invests money (capital) or human capital (may be debt or equity) in order to make more money.

The investors were as pleased as the owners when the small business won an important government contract.

See also: Capital, Human Capital, Investment, Profit

Invoice
A request for payment for products and services made by a business to its customers. Provides prices, terms, dates, and other information needed by the customer to pay the amount owed by an agreed-upon time.

The oil company left invoices for its customers with every oil delivery so people didn't need to be at home in order to pay at the time.

See also: Accounts Receivable, Customer, Payment, Terms

Issued Stock
Shares of stock sold or transferred to the stockholders from the authorized pool of stock.

The initial public offering broke records for issued stock sold in the first day of trading.

See also: Stockholder or Shareholder, Stock

J

Job Description
A summary of task requirements describing what a specific job entails.

Based on the job description, the woman was overqualified for the position, but she applied anyway because she thought it would be a fun job.

See also: Employee, Task

Jobber
A wholesale merchant who acts as a middleman, buying goods from manufacturers and then selling them to retailers.

Many auto parts jobbers now have e-commerce Web sites to improve efficiency and provide better service.

See also: Distribution, Distributor, Retailer, Wholesaling

Joint Venture
A legal entity formed between two or more parties to undertake economic activity together and collaboratively pursue a particular project or business, with a sharing of profits or losses.

The joint venture between the soft-drink company and the fast-food chain was highly profitable for both.

See also: Partnership, Strategic Alliances

Just-in-Time (JIT)

A concept used in manufacturing that requires parts to be ready only at the time they are needed in production and no earlier.

In spite of their initial skepticism, the plant managers discovered that changing to a just-in-time philosophy actually saved time and money and improved quality, resulting in happier customers.

See also: Outsourcing

K

Kaizen

A philosophy for achieving quality through continuous improvement by humanizing the workplace and eliminating hard work (both mental and physical). Teaches people and teams how to do rapid experiments using the scientific method and how to learn to see and eliminate waste in business processes.

As executives are realizing the importance of a strong, healthy, and happy workforce, the idea of Kaizen is becoming more prevalent in corporate America.

See also: Continuous Improvement, Quality, Teams, Total Quality Management (TQM)

Kanban

A management system to facilitate just-in-time manufacturing; frequently known as a "pull" system, as everything is pulled in response to past demand.

The plant reduced its storage needs once it moved to a Kanban system of manufacturing.

See also: Just-in-time, Lean Manufacturing, Production

Key Capabilities

The knowledge and skill required for a business to maintain its standing within its particular tier.

The new owners of the company assured the stockholders that nothing would be done to lose the key capabilities of the business at any time after the buyout so all investments were still safe.

See also: Core Competencies, Skill

Key Success Factors

The factors that are a necessary condition for success in a given market; the key things that can tell management when the organization or team has reached its goals.

The key success factors were clear enough for the company to track even during the industry upheaval.

See also: Critical Success Factors (CSFs), Goals, Management, Organizations, Teams

Keystone

A cost-based retail pricing policy by which a business doubles the cost of a product, resulting in 50 percent gross margin or 100 percent markup on cost.

The surplus store used a keystone pricing strategy for the dry-goods items on the shelves.

See also: Gross Margin, Markup

Keyword

A word or phrase used to perform a Web search using a search engine. Web sites emphasize important terms in their copy and meta tags, making their sites more likely to appear in the list of search results.

Often a keyword search is all a user needs to perform in order to find the desired information.

See also: Banners, Link, Meta Tags, World Wide Web (WWW)

Keyword Density

A ratio of keywords to total words on a Web page; used to determine whether keywords are being overused on a Web page. Keywords should fall into the 3 percent to 10 percent density range.

The Web site's keyword density was so high it actually made linking to the site less likely.

See also: Keyword, World Wide Web (WWW)

Kickback

The payment of something of value to another individual with the goal of persuading or influencing that person's decision or performance in certain situations; an illicit means of influencing how a contract is awarded.

The major construction company was promised a kickback from the small start-up for not bidding on the bridge project.

See also: Cash, Contract, Payments

Kickoff Meeting

A management meeting held at the end of major planning activities for all stakeholders to provide an overview of the project and outline expectations, to ensure a common understanding of the project, and to build consensus and excitement about the project, venture, task force, or new initiative.

The kickoff meeting included all the program directors and supervisors so that everyone received the same information, in the same way, at the same time.

See also: Communication, Meeting, Project, Stakeholders, Task

Killer Application

An innovative software product that makes a whole system or service successful in the marketplace; an application that surpasses all of its competitors, meeting marketplace demand and need.

The popularity of personal computers has given rise to several killer applications, such as e-mail, that cannot be matched by real-world competitors.

See also: Application, Competition, Competitive Advantage, Innovation, Software

Killing

A big profit.

Investors who bought stocks in the major computer companies have made a killing over the last few decades.

See also: Profit, Windfall

Kiosk

A booth or stand that holds a specific type of merchandise from or information about one company.

The kiosks outside the mall had to close every winter but were back in place by early spring.

See also: Brand, Marketing

Knowledge

Acquired competencies; the psychological result of perception, learning, and reasoning.

Although education is important, it is also important for employees to have the knowledge of the industry that can only come with hands-on experience.

See also: Competencies, Knowledge Management, Knowledge Workers, Knowledgeable

Knowledge Management
The practice of researching, collecting, and organizing an enterprise's employees' knowledge; capturing, organizing, and storing knowledge and experiences of individual workers and groups within an organization and making it available to others in the organization.

After the executives were replaced in the organization, the new CEO was wise enough to institute knowledge management in order to learn from the long-time employees.

See also: Expert System, Intellectual Capital, Knowledge, Organizations

Knowledge Workers
Managers, executives, and employees who work primarily with information or who develop and use knowledge in the work place; people with the ability to acquire and apply knowledge. A term coined by Peter Drucker in 1959.

National and international expansion has increased the need for knowledge workers in many corporations.

See also: Information, Knowledge Management

Knowledgeable
Well-informed; having information about or an understanding of.

The knowledgeable researcher is well acquainted with the research methods generally used by the company's research-and-development department.

See also: Knowledge Workers

Knowledgeware
A set of tools that helps companies easily capture, share, and reapply knowledge. By reusing valuable, existing corporate information, companies can optimize product lifecycle management and facilitate automated design.

The knowledgeware applications allowed designers to build on the most popular aspects of the car for each new version without making the same mistakes of the past.

See also: Information Management, Intangible Assets, Knowledge Management, Knowledge Workers, Life Cycle

Kudos
Credit given for an achievement or meeting a goal.

Although the award was in his name, the director gave kudos to his team during his acceptance speech.

See also: Goals, Rewards

L

Labor Pool

A source of trained personnel from which an employer can recruit.

Many firms consider Ivy League schools to be readymade labor pools from which to draw new employees.

See also: Employee, Recruiting

Laptop

A portable computer that can run on battery power and be connected to a wireless network.

The young writer enjoyed taking her laptop down to the coffee shop so she could work and people watch at the same time.

See also: Computer, Network, Personal Digital Assistant (PDA)

Last In First Out (LIFO)

An inventory management method in which the last goods purchased are assumed to be the first goods sold, so that the ending inventory consists of the first goods purchased.

One of the ways the business managed its cash flow was buy using a LIFO inventory management method.

See also: Current Assets, First In First Out (FIFO), Inventories, Purchase

Law of Large Numbers

States that if a group or cohort is large enough, one can predict outcomes.

The insurance company used the law of large numbers to predict how many of its clients would become severely ill over the course of a twelve-month period.

See also: Forecast, Outcome

Layoff

A period of inactivity in the workplace that results in an employee's separation from work. Usually the separation is a temporary one and is caused by factors outside the worker's control.

The steel workers understood they would face layoffs at least once a year but also knew their union would get them back to work as soon as possible.

See also: Rightsizing, Termination

Lead

A new prospect or client previously unknown to a salesperson or company; the identity of a person or entity potentially interested in purchasing a product or service. Acquiring leads represents the first stage of a sales process.

Although she was willing to follow up on established leads, she was not willing to make cold calls.

See also: Client, Customer, Customer Resource Management (CRM), Direct Marketing, Prospect

Lead Time

The anticipated amount of time to implement a plan; time needed to do the tasks and activities to bring a new product to market.

The computer glitch cut down on the lead time the team had for the new project, so it became a bit of a rush job.

See also: Just-in-Time, Product Development, Time-to-Market

Leadership

The ability to facilitate change and to unite followers in a shared vision that will improve an organization and society at large; activity of leading. Characteristic of an organization that leads its industry, segment, and market.

Strong leadership was more important than ever after the scandal involving the accounting division became national news.

See also: Authority, Followership, Market Leaders, Vision

Leadership Selection

A process of deciding on who will lead a team, organization or firm; a decision on a leader.

The leadership selection for each project was left up to the individual program directors.

See also: Leadership, Legacy, Succession

Leading Indicators

Those metrics that predict future economic activity in the United States.

The publication of leading indicators often triggers the stock market to rise or fall.

See also: Economics, Metrics

Lean Manufacturing

A systematic elimination of non–value-added efforts in a manufacturing process; a management process to improve quality and profitability at the same time.

Lean manufacturing processes have revolutionized the way many leading enterprises deliver products to their customers and manage their suppliers.

See also: Manufacturing, Quality, System

Lean Organization

An effective organization that strives for efficiency; a productive team.

The goal of the CEO was to reorganize the company in such a way that it became a lean organization instead of a wasteful one.

See also: Downsizing, Organizations, Rightsizing

Learning Curve

A way to show how long it takes for a person, team, or process to become efficient.

The young man was further along the learning curve than his contemporaries because he had learned much of the technique from his father, not just in school.

See also: Efficiency, Organizational Development, Period, Team Building

Learning Organization

Team and/or organization where people continually expand their capacity to create the results they truly desire, where new and expansive patterns of thinking are nurtured, where collective aspiration is set free, and where people are continually learning how to learn together; an organization where acquisition of knowledge is a key to success.

The new director hoped to make the department into a learning organization instead of allowing it to remain about completing paperwork and meeting quotas.

See also: Change, Change Management, Growth, Learning, Organizations, Teams

Lease

A contract by which a tenant (the "lessee") takes possession of office space, furniture, equipment, or other property for a specified rent and specified amount of time.

The entrepreneurs were excited to find a small shop to lease at a very reasonable price.

See also: Agreement, Contract, Period

Lease Financing

Financing the acquisition of plant or equipment by leasing rather than buying it.

The researchers used lease financing to get the equipment since they would only need it for a few tests.

See also: Assets, Financing, Lease

Lease Purchase Agreement

An agreement wherein part of the lessee's monthly rent is applied toward the purchase of the property. When the agreed equity is reached, the ownership is transferred to the lessee.

The artist had a lease purchase agreement on his studio because he knew he wanted to stay in the area but couldn't afford to buy the building right away.

See also: Agreement, Contract, Equity, Lease, Period, Purchase

Ledger

A book of accounts of a firm.

Only the accounting staff and the treasurer had access to the ledger.

See also: Accounting, Bookkeeping, General Ledger

Legacy

The transfer of power from one generation of leadership to another; or an existing or antiquated system that continues to be used past its intended or expected life.

The founder of the firm hoped to leave a legacy of environmentally friendly manufacturing when he finally retired.

or

Today, the typewriter is considered by many to be a legacy machine.

See also: Computer, Leadership, Network, Succession, System

Lender

An individual or financial institution that temporarily lends out money with the expectation that it will be repaid in full with interest.

The entrepreneurs tapped every lender who would meet with them in order to finance their dream.

See also: Banks, Interest, Loan

Lessee

The renter or tenant.

The property manager was responsible to the lessees as well as to the owner of the building.

See also: Lease, Lease Purchase Agreement, Lessor

Lessor

The landlord or owner.

The tenants could only change the building's appearance with written permission from the lessor.

See also: Lease, Lease Purchase Agreement, Lessee, Property

Letter of Credit

A binding document that a buyer can request from his or her bank in order to guarantee that the payment for goods will be transferred to the seller; a form of guarantee that a contractual obligation is met.

The city issued a large letter of credit payable to whatever company would come in and take over the old factory, hoping to bring business into the declining neighborhood.

See also: Bank, Contact

Letter of Intent (LOI)

A letter from one company to another acknowledging a willingness and ability to do business, usually nonbinding, before the agreement is finalized; a means of clarifying the key points of a complex transaction for the convenience of the parties.

The two companies signed the letter of intent prior to the merger.

See also: Negotiation, Term Sheet

Letter of Recommendation

A letter from an auditor to a client, evaluating the company's current accounting system and making recommendations on how to improve it.

Their auditor sent them a letter of recommendation with some changes that needed to be made prior to the next inspection.

See also: Accounting, Audit, Communication

Leverage

The advantage gained from using an existing resource or capability in a new market, or improving performance in a market currently served; or investing with borrowed money as a way to amplify potential gains.

The corporation used the leverage it had gained from the new MP3 player to move into aspects of the music software industry.

or

Using leveraged money to launch the new project was risky but everyone involved believed it was worth it.

See also: Leveraged Buyout (LBO)

Leveraged Buyout (LBO)

Purchase or takeover of a company using largely borrowed funds. The idea is for the buyers to be able to pay the funds back using the profits from the company once the sale is complete.

The investment manager refused to authorize a leveraged buyout of the smaller company because she was unable to verify that it would be profitable soon enough to pay off the debt.

See also: Acquisition, Debt, Leverage, Takeover

Liability

The financial obligations entered in the balance sheet of a business enterprise; something owed to another business or individual; a debt of the business; synonymous with legal responsibility.

The larger firm decided buying the smaller one was worth the liabilities it would bring to the table.

See also: Accounting, Assets, Balance Sheet, Debt, Obligation

Lien

A legal claim against property; security or payment for a debt or duty.

The homeowners were able to get a lien on the park because the driveway was laid before the lands had become protected.

See also: Debt, Payments

Life Cycle

The progression of a product through stages, from concept to decline.

Many high-tech toys are too expensive at the beginning of their life cycle for the average person to be able to afford them.

See also: Product Development, Product Life Cycle Management (PLM), Project Life Cycle

Limited Liability Company (LLC)

A type of business structure that allows the owners to be taxed as a partnership, but with the limited liability of a corporation.

The businessmen elected to form an LLC so that in the early years the losses offset their personal income taxes.

See also: Corporation, Liability, Partnership, Taxes

Limited Liability Partnership (LLP)

A type of partnership recognized in many states that protects individual partners from personal liability for negligent acts committed by other partners and employees not under their direct control.

Although the attorneys trusted each other, they all saw the wisdom in forming an LLP just in case.

See also: Corporation, Liability, Partnership, Taxes

Limited Partner

An individual who has limited liability in a partnership.

As a limited partner, she had very little say in the decisions that were made about the organization because she could not be part of the management team.

See also: Liability, Limited Liability Partnership (LLP), Partnership, Taxes

Limited Partnership

A form of partnership composed of both a general partner(s) and a limited partner(s); the limited partners have no control in the management of the company and are usually financially liable only to the extent of their investment in the partnership.

There was very little competition in the limited partnership among the partners because each played as much of a role as they wanted.

See also: General Partner, Limited Liability Partnership (LLP), Limited Partner

Line of Credit

Short-term financing usually granted by a bank up to a predetermined limit. The debtor borrows as needed up to the limit of credit without needing to renegotiate the loan.

The couple was approved for a $5,000 line of credit in order to make improvements on their house.

See also: Bank, Credit, Debt

Link

A channel for communication between groups, Web pages, networks, or organizations; text or images that, when clicked, take the user to another page or site.

The writer was thrilled when she was invited to link her Web page to the publishing house's home page.

See also: Communication, Computer, Hypertext, Network, Web Page, World Wide Web (WWW)

Liquid

The ease with which assets can be converted to cash; a measure of how quickly a stock can be converted to cash; the ratio of a business' assets that can be monetized.

Since she worked under contract instead of having a steady paycheck, the writer needed to keep her assets liquid in order to assure she could pay her bills on time.

See also: Assets, Capital, Cash, Monetize, Risk

Liquidation

The process of converting assets into cash.

Once the company went into liquidation, everything was sold.

See also: Assets, Cash, Liquid

Listening

Hearing what is being said in a constructive, focused manner.

Few business people understand the importance of simply setting aside personal agendas and listening to the information being offered.

See also: Communication

Loan

An agreement between two parties in which the lender transfers an item to the borrower with the expectation of the item being returned at a later date.

The loan the bank was willing to issue wasn't large enough to help the small start-up.

See also: Bridge Loan, Debt, Signature Loan, Term Loan, Unsecured Loan

Local Area Network (LAN)

The way businesses connect computers locally; a data communications network spanning a limited geographical area, usually a few miles at most, providing communications between computers and peripheral devices.

The small business was unable to allow staff to work from home because the LAN was so limited it didn't reach out of the downtown area.

See also: Data Communication, Network, Virtual Private Network (VPN), Wide Area Network (WAN), Wi-Fi

Log

A record of how something is used, a process is done, or a test is run.

The bottling team kept a log of the products they packaged and the raw material used to produce the products.

See also: Data, Database, Process

Logical

Being able to reason in an orderly way, drawing upon relevant fundamental points to reach or support a conclusion, determination, or solution.

The team approached the crisis in a logical and rational manner, so it was quickly resolved.

See also: Fuzzy Logic, Intuition, Leadership, Systematic

Logical Incrementalism

A planning methodology of management that relies on a gradual incremental approach to the decision-making process; a natural and intuitive way to tackle everyday problems.

The team used logical incrementalism to address concerns that were actually possible instead of wasting time finding solutions for issues that would probably not occur.

See also: Goal, Muddling Through, Organization, Problem Solving, Strategic Choices

Logistics

The management function of sourcing and distributing material and product in the proper place and in proper quantities at the appropriate time.

The logistics behind getting care packages to 400 families meant a nightmare for the staff, but it was worthwhile when the children smiled their thanks.

See also: Distribution, Sourcing, Transportation

Logo

A symbol that a company uses to represent itself or its brand.

Many teenagers are more likely to be able to recognize the logo of their favorite company than a picture of the vice president of the country.

See also: Brand, Marketing, Symbol

Longitudinal Study

Long-term market research and surveys based on repeated analysis of either the same group or sample (called a panel study) or new samples chosen at regular intervals. Tracking the same population makes it less likely that any differences observed in those people will be the result of cultural differences.

The Food and Drug Administration required a longitudinal study of patients taking the drug in trial before approving it for general consumption.

See also: Cohort, Focus Group, Group Interview, Market Research, Panels

Long-Term Debt

Debt, loans, or other credit instruments that are to be paid back over a period greater than a year.

People understand they are entering into long-term debt when they buy a house or car.

See also: Credit, Debt, Loan

Long-Term Liabilities

Debts of a business, other than current liabilities; that is, debts that are due at least one calendar year in the future or beyond the normal operating period.

The company was thriving, so no one was concerned about its ability to handle long-term liabilities.

See also: Balance Sheet, Liability, Long-Term Debt

Loss

The result of revenues being less than expenses.

The new restaurant operated at a loss for the first year.

See also: Expenses, Profit, Revenue

Loss Leader

A product or service sold at or below cost to attract customers for the remaining product line; a sales promotion.

She bought the loss leader once because of the sale but was so impressed that she was later willing to pay full retail for it.

See also: Product Line, Profit Margin, Promotion, Retailer, Sales

Low-Hanging Fruit

The task, sale, or customers that are easiest to target and that are therefore usually tackled first; an easily attainable objective. Usually the least costly transactions or the most accessible.

By dealing with the low-hanging fruit, the team felt productive and got off on a good start instead of becoming overwhelmed by the size of the project.

See also: Goals, Objectives, Task

Loyalty

Feelings of allegiance; the quality of being loyal.

A company or product doesn't need to be superior to its competitors in order to instill customer loyalty so long as it consistently meets other needs of the consumers.

See also: Allegiance, Customer, Customer Loyalty

M

Macroenvironmental Factors

An array of external macro-factors—fiscal policy and macroeconomic affects—influencing an enterprise's ability to achieve its mission, purpose, and objectives.

Taxation and international trade regulation are two macroenvironmental factors that the entrepreneurs considered in their business plan.

See also: Competitive Conditions, Competitive Landscape (Environment), Mission, PEST Analysis, SWOT Analysis

Management

The person or team in charge of an organization; those with the authority to make important decisions; the process or practice of managing.

The contentment, efficiency, and loyalty of a program's field staff can almost always be traced back to the skills, or lack thereof, of the management-level staff.

See also: Authority, Controlling, Decision Making, Direction, Leadership, Organization, Planning

Management by Objectives

A management style that outlines goals and objectives for employees and then later compares those with actual performance.

Once the nonprofit moved to management by objective, the entire staff was better able to understand the mission of the program and work more effectively toward helping their clients.

See also: Appraisal, Goals, Objectives, Performance

Management by Walking Around (MBWA)

A management technique in which executives and managers get out of their offices and both observe and talk to employees at locations where they work; listening to the troops.

The director was successful and well respected because she used the MBWA technique to assure her staff she was always available to them.

See also: Communication, Management, Participative Management

Management Effectiveness

The means by which management is measured; managerial accountability; how well a person manages those in his charge.

The board of directors will monitor the management effectiveness of all the executive officers so that even they are accountable to the stockholders.

See also: Accountability, Conflict Resolution, Delegation, Effectiveness, Execution, Leadership, Management, Performance

Management Information Systems (MIS)

A means of using computers to make better decisions and solving business problems with information technology.

Having a strong MIS department allows businesses to be more efficient and often more cost-effective.

See also: Decision Support Systems (DSS), Expert System, Management, Predictive Metrics

Management Philosophy

A way to manage a business; a set of principles to guide the management team in making decisions.

The CEO and the board of directors would only consider hiring management-level employees who shared their management philosophy.

See also: Management, Mission, Principles, Values

Management Team

A group of individuals who combine their talents to run an enterprise; the group charged with providing management to a business, project, or program as a mutually supportive team.

The management team met twice a month in order to ensure the whole department was running as well as necessary.

See also: Management, Organizations, Project, Team Building, Teams

Management Style

The approach a person takes to deal with people and organizations.

The program director's management style was so aggressive and punitive that she had a hard time keeping her staff from quitting.

See also: Collaborate, Culture, Leadership, Management

Manager

A person who plans, organizes, controls, and directs an organization, project, or venture.

A manager's job should be based on a task to be performed in order to attain the company's objectives.

See also: Controlling, Directing, Management, Planning, Project, Venture

Mandate

An authoritative order or requirement.

The government of the United States mandates that certain safety regulations be maintained in all businesses, regardless of industry, size, or location.

See also: Authority, Demand, Direction

Manifest

A detailed account of everything that is being transported. The manifest is put in a place that will be safe even in the event of an accident.

The manifest was checked on both ends of the delivery to ensure nothing was lost.

See also: Logistics, Transportation

Manipulation

An illegal practice that involves creating a false impression that the market is active by buying or selling securities.

The manipulation scandal involved traders at all levels of the company from the executives on down.

See also: Market, Security

Manufacturing

Transforming raw materials into something that provides value to a customer or user; a wealth-producing sector of an economy. The manufacturing effort includes all intermediate processes required for the production and integration of a product's components.

The success of the company allowed the plant to go from manufacturing 500 to 5,000 units in a day.

See also: Digital Manufacturing, Industry, Lean Manufacturing, Outsourcing

Marginal

Incremental; something or someone close to a lower limit.

Often, quality among similar projects made by different companies can run the gamut between marginal and exceptional.

See also: Edge, Marginal Cost, Marginal Revenue

Marginal Cost

Actual additional out-of-pocket cost of producing one more unit.

The marginal cost of producing one more widget was acceptable since the equipment was already running and staffed.

See also: Accounting, Advertising, Production

Marginal Revenue

The extra income received from selling one more unit.

The marginal revenue the printing company received for one more copy is surprisingly high.

See also: Marginal, Revenue

Markdown

A reduction in price (usually in connection with retail pricing).

After a holiday, customers often see markdowns on seasonal items that retailers make in order to sell those products quickly.

See also: Price, Retailer

Market

Total of all individuals or organizations that represent potential buyers; the demand for a product or service; a place where a product is sold.

The market for entertainment and recreation will never dry up, as was proven during both Prohibition and the Great Depression.

See also: Buyers, Demand

Market Challenger

A firm in a strong but not dominant position that is following an aggressive strategy of trying to gain market share.

Shortly after going national, the younger company became an unexpected market challenger to the well-established chain.

See also: Market Follower, Market Leaders

Market Development

A market growth strategy that seeks to expand a firm's reach into undeveloped markets such as new geographical markets, new distribution channels, different pricing policies, innovative packaging, or creating new market segments.

The fall of the USSR was an excellent opportunity for market development for any entrepreneur willing to take the chance.

See also: Brand, Distribution, Marketing

Market Factors

External forces or; influences on strategic choices through changes in the industry. Market factors impact the timing and positioning of products and programs that are in the firm's portfolio.

The failure of the venture was caused by the development team not considering all the market factors in play.

See also: Competitive Advantage, Competitive Pressure, Strategic Success Factors (SSFs)

Market Follower

A business that tends to stay in a position behind the leader in the market without challenging that leadership position; risk-adverse market position.

The iced-tea company was more than happy to remain a market follower as the competition between the two leading soft-drink companies heated up.

See also: Market Challenger, Market Leaders, Niche Player

Market Leaders

The dominant players in an industry; companies with major market share in a segment or industry; companies in a position to control price, distribution, and position.

The market leaders in most industries are easily identified by well-known brands, ad campaigns, or even spokespeople.

See also: Industry, Market Challenger

Market Penetration

A growth strategy in which the business focuses on selling existing products into existing markets; a focus on changing incidental clients to regular clients and regular client into heavy clients.

The expansion of the store was geared toward national market penetration.

See also: Growth, Marketing, Penetration Pricing, Skimming the Cream, Strategy

Market Research

A collection of facts about an industry, customers, an area, and a business; collecting new data to solve a marketing information need. Primary information acquisition when it's gathered for a particular purpose. Secondary when it's already been gathered about a business or industry.

Many successful ad campaigns were the result of strategic market research.

See also: Focus Group, Served Available Market, Total Available Market (TAM)

Market Share

A measurement for how dominant a company is in its industry; the percentage of the total market (or industry) sales made by one firm. As a formula, market share equals a firm's sales divided by total market sales.

Although they knew the smaller company would never overtake the larger corporations, the investors were pleased when its market share rose several points.

See also: Metrics, Served Available Market (SAM), Total Available Market (TAM)

Marketability
The ease with which a product or service can be sold; ability to quickly convert property to cash at minimal cost.
The marketability of high-priced luxury goods dropped after the oil crash in the 1980s.
See also: Market, Marketing

Marketing
An organizational function and a set of processes for creating, communicating, and delivering value to customers and for managing customer relationships in ways that benefit the organization and its stakeholders.
The firm extended its marketing to diverse communities and immediately saw sales increase.
See also: Communication, Market Share, Market, Sales, Stakeholders

Marketing Plan
A plan for packaging and selling products and services thus increasing sales to the customer or end user; a method for an organization to build markets, brands, and increase penetration in key segments. Often a section in a business plan.
Businesses will often reevaluate their marketing plans if sales drop unexpectedly, especially in a strong economy.
See also: Brand, Business Plan, Marketing, Strategy

Markup
Amount added to the cost of a product or service to determine its retail price.
Every store adds a markup to products in order to turn a profit on the goods sold.
See also: Initial Markup, Keystone, Markdown, Retailer, Sales

Mass Production
Producing standardized items in large quantities, usually involving automation, robotics, or specialized equipment.
Artists are often against the mass production of their work because they fear a loss of quality and originality.
See also: Manufacturing, Production, Productivity

Matrix Organization
An organization in which project team members answer to both a functional manager and a project manager.
Working in a matrix organization can be challenging unless both managers involved are on the same page and working on the same timeline.
See also: Decentralized, Functional, Organizations, Structure, Teams, Top-Down

Mature

Displaying the qualities of an experienced, well-developed adult; a person with this characteristic brings much deliberation to the processes of decision making and problem solving.

The new project leader was a mature, seasoned manager who could interact with subordinates in a calm, self-assured way.

See also: Decision Making

Maturity

The period and date when payment of a loan is due. As applied to securities and commercial loans, the period and date when payment of principal is due.

When at all possible, it is wise to pay off loans prior to their maturity date in order to avoid paying some of the penalties.

See also: Loan, Payment

Mean

The sum of the values for all observations of a variable divided by the number of observations.

While knowing the mean results can be important to making decisions about customers, one must never forget that there is a person behind each number and that humans can't be predicted like equations.

See also: Analysis, Metrics, Six Sigma

Measurement

The act or process of comparing results to requirements; assigning numbers or labels to things in accordance with specific rules to represent quantities or qualities of attributes; an objective, quantitative estimate of performance.

Measurements are important to providing people with feedback on how a team is performing and where they could improve.

See also: Metrics, Performance, Process, Variance

Media

The various avenues of communications; means used by the transmitter of a message to deliver it to the intended receiver in a communications system. In advertising, refers to newspaper, radio, television, magazines, billboard, direct mail, Internet, and other such outlets used to carry advertisements.

For many small firms on tight budgets, the Internet and AM radio are the primary advertising media.

See also: Advertising, Communication

Media Buyer
A person who plans for the purchase of space and time for advertising in appropriate formats and outlets (television, print, Internet) for various companies.
A great media buyer will know where to by banner ads and who to target.
See also: Advertising, Buyer, Marketing, Media

Mediation
A form of alternative dispute resolution in which a neutral party (the mediator) seeks to promote and negotiate a settlement between opposing parties in a dispute. There is no mechanism to compel the parties to settle; they must voluntarily agree to any settlement.
The firm hoped the disgruntled employees would agree to mediation rather than taking the harassment suit to court.
See also: Agreement, Settlement

Mediocrity
Ordinariness as a consequence of being average and not outstanding.
It is the desire to avoid mediocrity that drives many people to be willing to risk failing spectacularly.
See also: Leadership, Management, Meritocracy, Motivation

Meeting
The act of coming together for a business purpose; a formally arranged gathering of a team or organization to communicate.
Some days it feels as if the entire shift is made up of meetings but very little gets accomplished.
See also: Communication, Organization, Teams

Memorandum (Memo)
An informal note used to communicate information within an organization.
The director sent a memo to all the departments reminding them of the upcoming holiday.
See also: Communication, Credit Memo, Offering Memorandum

Mentor

A leader who is willing and able to coach or counsel a less capable person; or to provide guidance and support to facilitate the advancement and professional development of another.

The firm created a program in which senior partners would act as mentors to the junior associates.

or

When entering a new profession, it is helpful to have someone more experienced in the field to mentor and guide you.

See also: Coaching, Facilitator

Menu

A selection of possible choices and preferences provided by computer software.

Most word-processing commands can be found in a drop-down menu.

See also: Choices, Computer, Preferences, Software

Merchandise

Products sold at the retail level.

New merchandise was stocked every Tuesday afternoon, so many shoppers came in on Wednesdays.

See also: Product, Seconds

Merchant Account

An industry term for a business banking relationship whereby you and a bank have arranged to accept credit card payments (usually, a local bank can suffice for this kind of relationship). Facilitates business to accept credit cards, debit cards, gift cards, and other forms of electronic payment.

Due to the fees charged by merchant accounts, many stores have a minimum accepted amount for charge sales.

See also: Banks, Credit Card, Debit Card, E-Commerce, Internet, Web Page

Merger

The act of two or more companies pooling their resources to form a consolidated business. Achieved by offering the stockholders in one company securities in the acquiring company in exchange for the surrender of their stock.

The merger between the two companies brought together the strengths of both, thus creating a powerhouse in the industry.

See also: Acquisition, Mergers and Acquisitions (M&A), Strategy, Stockholder or Shareholder

Mergers and Acquisitions (M&A)

A term used by business and investment bankers to describe the strategy and management process dealing with the merging and acquiring of different businesses as well as other assets.

The investor looked closely at the company's history of M&A before deciding to back the latest one.

See also: Due Diligence, Merger, Synergy

Merit Increase

A wage increase given to a worker in recognition of a good job performance.

The staff was eligible for merit increases every six months, so they were motivated to perform well.

See also: Compensation, Wage

Meritocracy

A management philosophy based on ability, competence, and talent. Promotions in this type of system are a result of competition and demonstrated performance and reward talent, knowledge, motivation, and capability.

The system of meritocracy meant that staff worked harder and produced higher-quality results.

See also: Ability, Competencies, Competition, Leadership, Organization

Meta Tags

Specialized tags in the section of a Web page that provides indexing and descriptive keywords to help search engines catalog a firm's site.

The meta tags are one of the most important factors to consider when making a Web site accessible during a search.

See also: Link, Search Engine, Web Page

Methodology

A sequence of steps or a predefined process put in place by management that is meant to increase the organizational effectiveness; recommended practices; the rationale and the philosophical assumptions that underlie a particular study; or the approach a moderator uses to conduct focus groups.

The research methodology required in the lab was strict but clear cut so no one could claim ignorance.

or

She declined the opportunity to run the focus group because she was uncomfortable with the methodology requested by the department.

See also: Market Research, Organizations, Project Management

Metrics

An economic tool that measures the performance of companies, operations, projects, or others against competitors or industry standards; a means of telling a story by determining the value that describes some aspect of a business. This value purports to provide a prediction or estimate of the usability of the business and aid management in allocating resources, monitoring intent, and performance.

According to the metrics provided to the management team, the project was far ahead of similar ones approaching completion.

See also: Measurement, Ratio Analysis

Mezzanine Financing

A layer of money, either debt or equity, provided after the initial investment but still during the early growth stages, to finance operations until the firm is ready to go to market for its long-run financing.

The entrepreneurs grew their manufacturing business using mezzanine financing for working capital.

See also: Debt, Equity, Financing, Growth, Growth Stage

Microeconomics

Economic analysis of particular components of the economy, such as the growth of a single industry or demand for a single product.

Analysts use microeconomics to explain how buyers make decisions about purchases and savings.

See also: Economics, Growth

Milestone

The completion of a significant event or major deliverable used to measure project progress; one of a series of numbered markers placed along a project network at regular intervals showing results.

Using milestones to track the progress of a project is an efficient and clear way to ensure everyone stays on schedule.

See also: Program Evaluation and Review Techniques (PERT)

Milking

Using a situation to one's full advantage; process of extracting other sources out of a single source, such as a news article, to create further leads and contacts.

The sales rep was known for milking her contacts in order to make her quotas.

See also: Advantage, Resource

Mindset

A set of assumptions, methods, or notations held by one or more people, teams, or groups of people, which is so established that it creates a powerful incentive within these people or groups to continue to adopt or accept prior behaviors, choices, or tools.

The mindset behind the merger was that the two companies could basically control the Northeast market if they joined forces.

See also: Assumptions, Behavior, Beliefs, Vision

Minority Shareholder

A shareholder whose voting ownership in a public company is less than 50 percent.

The corporation was also a minority shareholder in several other businesses.

See also: Stockholder or Shareholder, Stock

Mission

The core reasons for a business's existence; an organization's basic function in society, in terms of the products and services it produces as well as its means of creating and servicing customers.

Over time, the organization's mission evolved from helping the community to helping the region at large.

See also: Purpose, Strategy, Values

Moderator

A leader of a discussion, panel, or focus group that presides over the venue, forum, or debate.

The anchorman was invited to be the moderator for the presidential debate because he was known to be coolheaded and nonpartisan.

See also: Facilitator, Focus Group, Panels

Monetize

To convert into money; establish as legal tender; convert assets into cash.

Although the small company preferred not to, it did have to monetize its assets several times during the first five years in order to stay afloat.

See also: Assets, Cash

Monopoly

The exclusive control by one company of a product or service; the situation that obtains when a single company provides a certain kind of product or service, allowing the company to exert control over prices and limit competition.

When the U.S. government broke up the telephone monopoly, many smaller providers were able to enter the market.

See also: Economics, Competition, Monopsony, Oligopoly, Substitute

Monopsony

A market with one buyer and many sellers, in which the buyer is able to control price by varying the quantity purchases.

The most well-known monopsony is the U.S. Department of Defense, which contracts with several different companies for technology and material.

See also: Economics, Elasticity, Microeconomics, Monopoly

Mortgage

Giving legal title to secure the repayment of a loan; a written conveyance of real property made by the mortgagee (lender) to the business.

For many people, qualifying for a mortgage is an intimidating but worthwhile process.

See also: Assets, Lender, Loan, Payments

Motivate

Give an incentive for action; promote goal-directed behavior.

The CEO was smart enough to realize that a word of encouragement or congratulations when things went well could motivate her staff just as well as scolding when things went badly.

See also: Behavior, Motivation, Team Building

Motivated

Moved to act or perform, particularly by an incentive. One may be self-motivated or motivated by something.

The friendly competition between departments kept everyone motivated and therefore increased sales.

See also: Leadership, Motivation, Team Building

Motivation

The encouragement that provides a reason for someone to do something. A concept used to describe the factors within an individual, team, or organization that arouse, maintain, and channel behavior toward a goal. Another way to say this is that motivation produces goal-directed behavior.

The inventor's motivation to create the new technology stemmed from his volunteer work at the children's hospital.

See also: Behavior, Goals, Motivated, Organizational Behavior

Muddling Through

The notion that altering policy in small steps is more effective than by strategic change or strategic planning.

The project was so large that it was agreed that muddling through was preferable to implementing all the changes at once.

See also: Strategy

Multimedia

The use of multiple formats with information content to enhance the viewer's experience; use of digital media to store and experience interactive content such as text, audio, graphics, animation, and video.

Nearly all presentations have a multimedia component these days.

See also: Advertising, Presentation Graphics, Visual Aid

N

Near-Term Market

A relatively brief opportunity (lasting six to eighteen months) for a product or service to have value in the market before technological obsolescence or changing consumer demand eliminates it.

With the rapid change in technology, most digital products are near-term market items.

See also: Markets, Obsolescence, Opportunities, Product Obsolescence, Technical Obsolescence

Negotiation

An exchange of information for the purpose of defining the terms governing the exchange of goods (which may be information); a process whose objective is agreement that involves two or more agents who communicate for the purpose of exchanging some goods and defining the terms of the exchange.

Production stopped entirely when the negotiation process between management and the union stalled.

See also: Conflict Resolution

Net

The amount that remains after all charges and deductions are subtracted from a gross amount.

An employee's net pay is usually noticeably less than the base salary would indicate.

See also: Deduction

Net Present Value (NPV)

A metric used by businesses to help decide whether to proceed with a project, acquisition, or capital investment; the value of all future cash flows discounted in today's dollars at the enterprise's weighted average cost of capital (WACC) or the cost of capital (discount rate) determined by the weighted average, at market value, of the cost of all financing sources in the business enterprise's capital structure.

Although funding for the movie seemed like a good idea, after the hurricane and the lead actor's sudden illness, the negative net present value caused the backers to remove their support.

See also: Discount Rate, Discounted Cash Flow, Free Cash Flow, Time Value of Money

Net Profit

Profit from revenue minus cost of goods and expenses.

The store's net profits were high enough that month for the owner to take his staff to lunch in order to celebrate.

See also: Cost of Goods Sold (COGS), Expenses, Profit, Revenue

Net Revenue (Sales)

Sales value minus variable selling and distribution expenses; revenue generated from the sale of all the company's products or services, minus an allowance for returns, rebates, and so on. Reported on the income statement.

The net revenue was lower than expected going into the summer, but the store owner had faith it would rise after the tourist season.

See also: Gross Sales, Income Statement

Net Worth

Value or worth of the business owner(s) investment plus retained earnings; the difference between assets and liabilities; determined on the balance sheet by subtracting liabilities from assets. Net worth is also called equity.

The old woman lived so simply that people were shocked to learn her net worth was so high.

See also: Assets, Balance Sheet, Liability, Retained Earnings

Netiquette

Commonly accepted rules of behavior and communication using Internet services; a code of conduct that governs behavior on the Internet.

Although using abbreviations is acceptable when instant messaging, netiquette indicates more care should be taken when composing an e-mail.

See also: E-Commerce, E-Mail, Group Discussion, Internet, Spam

Network

A group of people who have some kind of commercial relationship; the act of exchanging information and establishing personal connections; the common channels established with important people in a variety of related fields to provide information and contacts which can be used to help the entrepreneur become successful; or the interconnection of computers to facilitate sharing of information and data.

Business professionals must be careful how often they call on their network for favors and be sure to reciprocate whenever given the opportunity.

or

Since the computer virus was so virulent, the IT department shut down the whole network until it could be quarantined.

See also: Communication, Computers, Information, Internet, Relationships, Virtual Private Network (VPN), Wide Area Network, World Wide Web (WWW)

New Entrants

Additional competitors in a given industry. Generally, new entrants raise the level of competition, thereby reducing the industry's attractiveness.

The new entrants into the computer industry quickly saturated the market to the point that several companies ended up going under.

See also: Entry Barriers, Porter's Five-Force Model

New Issue

A security sold by a company for the first time.

The media and financial news reported on the expected new issue for weeks before it actually went on sale.

See also: Exchanges, Initial Public Offering (IPO), Security

New York Stock Exchange (NYSE)

An marketplace where stocks are traded, the oldest US market for stock trading.

Although a busy place of business, the NYSE is also a tourist stop for many people visiting the city for the first time.

See also: Exchange, Stock

Niche Player

A focus strategy employed by a company that selectively operates in the small segment of a market in which it feels strongly competitive; alternatively, the company may concentrate on a select few target markets.

Although she didn't think she had the skills to take on a national company, the young woman knew her store could be a powerful niche player in the region.

See also: Market Challenger, Market Dominance, Market Follower, Market Leaders

Nomenclature

Terms, words, and phrases that are used in a particular market, segment, or industry.

When he changed careers, he had to learn a whole new nomenclature in order to discuss his new industry.

See also: Business Literacy, Terminology, Terms

Nondisclosure Agreement (NDA)

A contract that binds a person or business to maintaining the confidentiality of proprietary information or trade secrets and that prohibits disclosure of such information without authorization.

The nondisclosure agreement was still enforceable for three years after employees left the company.

See also: Agreement, Confidentiality, Disclosure, Trade Secret

Nonexempt Employee

Employees who are protected by standard wage and overtime laws that mandate payment for every hour of overtime worked.

As a nonexempt employee, she often volunteered for overtime in order to pad her paycheck.

See also: Employee

Nonprofit Corporation (Not-for-profit)

A corporation formed to provide activities and services for society (rather than profit for the stockholders). These organizations are exempt from corporate income taxes, and donations to these groups may be tax deductible.

Many nonprofit corporations exist to help people or communities in need.

See also: Corporation, Grant, Organizations, Stockholder or Shareholder, Taxes

O

Objections

Reasons for postponing or not making a decision; expressed opposition, or the reasons or causes for expressing opposition.

The investors' objections to the venture were resolved when they saw the reactions of the test group.

See also: Acquisition, Buyer, Decision Making, Sales, Takeover

Objective

The ability to give equal consideration to all possible solutions to a problem; able to consider the facts without being influenced by feelings, biases, or unfounded preconceptions.

It was difficult for members of the board to be objective when discussing raises for the CEO because, while they admired him as a businessman, they disliked him personally.

See also: Problem Solving

Objectives

Statements of expected results, ends, and achievements that transform goals into strategic thrusts and in turn into action plans.

Generally, companies with clear objectives will achieve greater success than those with only a vague concept of where they want to go.

See also: Corporate Objectives, Functional Objectives

Obligation

The state of being responsible to do or pay something; requirements that are to be fulfilled. A legal agreement specifying a payment or action and the penalty for failure to comply.

The director felt an obligation to praise her staff because she knew their good work made her look like a strong leader.

See also: Accountability, Debt, Payment

Observant

Watchful; mentally alert, quick to notice.

Since she was a skilled and observant attorney, she was able to recognize when the negotiations began to fall apart before either side was fully aware of it.

See also: Mindful

Obsolescence

The state of being out of date. Results from a change in the market that renders a product or service useless; as a result, there is no longer a demand for the product or service.

Part of the role of research and development is to have a new product available before the previous ones enter into obsolescence.

See also: Change, Commoditization, Demand, Life Cycle, Near-Term Market, Product Obsolescence, Technical Obsolescence

Obstacle

Barrier to success; a thing that stands between current reality and a goal.

Overhead costs can be an obstacle to ever getting a business up and running.

See also: Barrier, Goals, Success

Offering Memorandum

A summary of the terms and key provisions of a private or public offering to obtain financing. This document discusses products or services provided, competition, operations, management, workforce, marketing and sales strategies, and the history of the business.

The plan for transferring the funds was spelled out in the offering memorandum.

See also: Financing, Private Equity, Public Offering

Offshoring

Sending work, plants and/or jobs to another country entirely, the restructuring of a supply chain where one company relies on its supplier for functions that were previously performed in-house.

Many large corporations have been accused of damaging the economy because of their patterns of offshoring rather than keeping plants open in the United States.

See also: Globalization, Outsourcing, Supply Chain

Oligopoly

A form of market economy in which the number of buyers is small while the number of sellers in theory could be large; a few buying firms dominate a market and often control price and margins.

The principles of free trade and capitalism cannot exist in an oligopoly because the existing companies would simply band together to prevent new companies from forming or being successful.

See also: Economics, Elasticity, Market, Microeconomics, Monopoly, Monopsony

One-Time Cost/Expense

An expenditure related to doing business that is expected to occur only one time, usually at start-up. Also called a non-reoccurring cost.

The project required a significant one-time cost to get the Web site up and running.

See also: Project, Start-Up

Ongoing Cost

An expenditure related to doing business that is expected to occur on a regular and repeating basis.

The rent was their largest ongoing cost for running the surf shop.

See also: Cash Flow, Operating Expense, Variable Cost

Online

Operation of a computer while connected to a network.

She was connected online through a wireless network.

See also: Network, World Wide Web (WWW)

Open-Book Management

A simple yet very powerful approach to managing a business by giving employees all relevant financial information about the company so they can make better decisions as workers and think like businesspeople.

The open-book management style taught everyone, even the low-level employees, to think in terms of the company as a whole.

See also: Communication, Financial Literacy, Motivation, Team Building, Teams

Open Source

Software built and distributed without charge.

Everyone is allowed to download open source operating systems from the Internet.

See also: Application, Innovation, Software, Technology

Operating Budget

A financial plan outlining how a company will use its resources over a specified period of time.

During lean times, the operating budget of a business may be very different from what it was only a few years previously.

See also: Budget, Operations, Planning

Operating Expense

Normal costs to running a business, such as sales, general and administrative, overhead, salaries, rent, product development, and marketing.

With growing operating expenses, the management team decided to consolidate all the sales into one location.

See also: Expenses, Operations

Operating Income

A company's or organization's earnings from its core operations after it has deducted the cost of goods sold and general operating expenses. Operating income equals gross profit minus general operating expenses minus depreciation expense.

The accountants were pleased to report that the operating income for the shop had increased every quarter.

See also: Depreciation, Gross Profit, Operating Expense

Operating Manual

A guidebook on how to use a product or system.

The help-desk workers kept the operating manuals for all the different computer systems close at hand.

See also: Customer Service, Product

Operating Margin

A measurement of how well a company is managing its overhead costs. The equation for finding the operating margin is the gross margin minus the fixed production costs.

The first suggestion made by the consultant was regarding ways to decrease the operating margin in order to have more money going back into the business.

See also: Metrics, Overhead

Operations

Activities associated with providing services or products to customers; includes machining, packaging, assembly, equipment maintenance, testing, and all other value-creating activities that transform inputs into the final product.

The brokerage firm ran all its operations with the highest possible ethical standards.

See also: Product, Production

Operations Management

Managing the day-to-day activities of the enterprise; management of the actual businesses or profit centers of an enterprise, as opposed to staff functions, such as the legal, accounting, and public relations departments.

Generally, the chief operating officer is in charge of operations management allowing the chief executive officer to focus on strategy.

See also: Chief Operating Officer (COO), Management, Operations

Opportunities

Challenges for leadership to use resources, assets, and capabilities in new and different forms; new business projects and programs with possibility of creating value by creating new products or customers.

The philanthropist was always ready to hear about new opportunities that might be a good investment.

See also: Customer, Product, Program, Project, Resource Allocation, Strategy, SWOT Analysis, Value Creation

Opportunity Cost

The possibilities given up or forfeited by choosing to do one project over another one. Related to the time value of money by the trade-off between money now and money later. Depends, among other things, on the rate of interest you can earn by investing and the quality of the venture or project.

The team decided the opportunity cost of allocating advertising funds to online ads rather than traditional print media was worth the risk of losing the magazine readers.

See also: Project, Time Value of Money, Trade-Off, Venture

Options

Choices or selections; a number of things from which only one can be chosen; or a right to purchase something within a given time period at an agreed price.

The magazine offered several size and design options for ads placed within its pages.

See also: Stock Option, Strategic Choices

Oral Presentations

In-person discussion of some topic; a primary communication means of providing information and soliciting feedback.

Although she was comfortable on the phone and one on one, the thought of giving oral presentations to potential clients made her very nervous.

See also: Briefing, Communications, Elevator Pitch, Flipchart

Organizational Behavior

The way people behave inside a team or organization, often a topic of specialized study; the system of culture, leadership, communication, and group dynamics that determines an organization's actions.

The organizational behavior consultants started their analysis with a survey of employee perceptions.

See also: Behavior, Communication, Culture, Group Processes, Motivation, Organizations, Team

Organizational Capacity

The methods and means to grow and develop an organization to produce more.

Even though the company was small, its organizational capacity made it an excellent long-term investment.

See also: Capacity, Collaboration, Organizations

Organizational Chart

A diagram outlining the chain of command that makes up the structure of a business, showing specific areas of responsibility.

Every new employee was given an organizational chart as part of his or her hiring package.

See also: Organizations, Responsibility, Structure

Organizational Culture

The set of important assumptions that members of an organization share; the written and unwritten rules that shape and reflect the way an organization operates; overall attitudes and approaches by a company to conducting business, including handling of employees, suppliers, and customers.

Since the 1980s, there has been a shift in many organizational cultures from profit being most important to social accountability being equally important.

See also: Behavior, Communication, Culture, Group Processes, Motivation, Organizational Behavior, Organizations, Team

Organizational Development

Skills and techniques directed at interventions in the processes of human systems for the development and empowerment of teams and individuals (formal and informal groups, organizations, communities, and societies) in order to increase their effectiveness and health using a variety of disciplines, principally applied behavioral sciences.

After the merger, the firm brought in an organizational development specialist to assist with the transition.

See also: Change, Change Management, Human Capital, Organizations, Teams

Organizational Effectiveness

The ability of an organization to fulfill its mission through a blend of sound management, strong governance, and a rededication to achieving results.

The conflicts among the management team prevented the program's organizational effectiveness from being as sound as it should have been.

See also: Ability, Effectiveness, Organizational Behavior, Organizational Culture, Results

Organizational Planning

Outlining and managing the way that goals and objectives will be achieved; defining team member responsibilities, roles, and reporting structure, and preparing the staffing management plan.

After the department missed a major deadline, the director brought in an organizational planning specialist to ensure it never happened again.

See also: Goals, Objectives, Organizational Structure, Organizing, Planning, Teams

Organizational Structure

The means for implementing a plan, vision, or strategy through people; the pattern of how power, authority, and functions are distributed in any established group of people.

The organizational structure of the new department was explained clearly in the diagram presented to the board of directors.

See also: Authority, Functions, Organizations, Structure

Organizations

The way businesses and managers get things done; a formal group of people with one or more shared goals; a means to an end in order to achieve its goals.

Leaders can help their organizations to attain effectiveness by first recognizing the barriers and obstacles, then guiding their team around, over, or to remove the barrier.

See also: Organizational Development, Organizational Behavior, Teams, Virtual Organizations

Organized

Able to systematically arrange items, details, functions, or other elements in a logical, integrated manner; structured and orderly.

The team was organized enough that even when their deadline was moved up a week, they were still able to complete the project.

See also: Systematic

Other Expenses

Expenses or losses not related to primary business operations.

The firm subleased space to another business, accounting for the maintenance costs as other expenses.

See also: Accounting, Expenses, Income Statement, Operations

Other Income/Revenue

Income generated outside the normal scope of a company's typical operations; includes ancillary activities such as foreign currency gains.

Once the firm rented out the empty facility, their other income rose enough to cover the added cost of maintaining the space.

See also: Income, Operations, Period, Revenue

Out-of-Pocket Expense

Expenses incurred by an individual on a business trip that are paid for from the employee's personal funds.

Employees were encouraged to keep track of their out-of-pocket expenses and submit receipts for reimbursement.

See also: Expenses

Outcome

A result of a task, project, meeting, or activity.

Everyone in the lab knew that the problem would have to be solved before they could reach the outcome necessary for completing the project.

See also: Results

Outplacement

A means for facilitating the re-employment of terminated workers, employees, and executives through professional services and counseling at the employer's expense.

The company created an outplacement office when the decision to close was made so that staff could have assistance in finding new work.

See also: Downsizing, Severance

Outsourcing

Contracting of outside help to perform a particular task or an ongoing operation to gain cost effectiveness. Usually companies outsource activities like IT, mail, or food service—activities peripheral to their core business.

The shipping company decided outsourcing its IT department was more financially feasible than having several people on staff full-time.

See also: Operations

Overdraft

A check drawn for a larger amount than the check writer has on deposit.

The contractor always made sure his clients' checks cleared before paying his workers in order to avoid an overdraft.

See also: Cash, Deposit

Overdue

A situation in which an invoice is beyond a due date for payment or a return.

His car payment was overdue because of the unexpected medical bills he had to pay earlier in the month.

See also: Invoice, Payments

Overhead

Operating cost indirectly associated with a product or its marketing, such as rent, executives' salaries, or administrative expenses.

The small firm didn't make enough money to cover the overhead incurred by being located downtown.

See also: Operating Costs

Overnight Delivery

A service promising delivery of packages by a designated time on the next business day.

Part of the store's continued success was its guaranteed overnight delivery procedure.

See also: Deadlines, Schedule, Transportation

Overrun

A production run that is more than what is needed; printed material or other manufactured product that exceeds the amount ordered.

The printer produced an overrun of the flyers in case some got damaged during the collating process.

See also: Inventories, Manufacturing, Production

Overtime

Hours worked in excess of the normal work week.

He didn't mind working overtime because he was paid time and a half for the extra hours.

See also: Contract, Employee, Period

P

Pacesetter

A leader; something that blazes trails in an industry and is widely copied.

The computer company's new technologies quickly made it the pacesetter in the industry, with all the competitors scrambling to catch up.

See also: Leadership

Packaging

The physical way a product/service is boxed or otherwise presented for merchandising, marketing, and distribution purposes.

A product's packaging can be as important in attracting new customers as the product itself.

See also: Distribution, Marketing

Packing List

A list that contains all the contents of a shipping container, box, or boxes.

The inventory came with a packing list to ensure everything that was supposed to be shipped arrived at the store.

See also: Delivery, Purchase Order

Padding

The practice of including expenses in an invoice or expense account that were outside the guidelines.

The young salesman submitted an expense for a family dinner, thus padding his expense account.

See also: Expenses, Guidelines, Invoice

Paid-In Capital

Capital received from investors in exchange for stock. Reported on the balance sheet.

After the initial buying frenzy when the company first went public, the paid-in capital leveled off and became a small, if consistent, part of the budget.

See also: Balance Sheet, Financial Statement or Reports, Stock

Panels

A group of experts gathered to discuss a topic, conduct group interviews, or to explore an issue; usually led by a facilitator or moderator.

The panel on global warming was made up of some of the greatest environmental and business minds in the country.

See also: Facilitator, Focus Group, Group Discussion, Interview, Longitudinal Study, Moderator

P

Paradigm Shift

A fundamental change in a major aspect of a business situation or marketplace that describes the process and result of a change in basic assumptions within the ruling theory and conventional wisdom. This new way of looking at something may be caused by innovations in technology, science, or any other factor influencing a situation.

The success of the Internet and e-commerce created a global paradigm shift in which all companies and corporations must now do business.

See also: Change

Paradox

An apparently true statement or group of statements that leads to a contradiction or a situation that defies intuition. Often used incorrectly as a synonym for contradiction. While a contradiction by definition cannot be true, many paradoxes do allow for resolution.

The paradox discovered in the lab had to be addressed before the project could move forward.

See also: Market, Strategic Thinking, Strategy

Parameter

A set quantity; any factor that defines a system and determines (or limits) its performance.

The CEO challenged his staff to stretch the parameters of the industry and what customers expected in terms of quality and service.

See also: Performance, System

Parent Company

A company that owns a majority stake (51 percent or more) of another company's shares.

People don't always realize that several of their favorite businesses are owned by a single parent company.

See also: Company, Control, Stockholder or Shareholder, Shares, Transfer Pricing

Pareto Chart

A graph that is used to rank the importance of a problem by the frequency with which it occurs.

The CCO's presentation included a Pareto chart showing the production problems and issues.

See also: Pareto's Law or Principle

Pareto's Law or Principle

The law of the vital few and the principle of factor sparsity; states that for many phenomena, 80 percent of the consequences stem from 20 percent of the causes. The Pareto principle, also known as the 80-20 rule, is used by managers to set goals and develop priorities.

No one familiar with Pareto's principle was surprised that the one issue caused so many problems with production.

See also: Pareto Chart, Quality Control, Six Sigma

Parkinson's Law

Rule stating that work expands to fill the time available for its completion. Frequently used by managers to set goals, timelines, and milestones.

True to Parkinson's law, the project that could have been completed in five days took the ten the contract had granted.

See also: Goals, Milestone

Participative Management

Leadership style in which workers are encouraged to give opinions and participate in meeting where plans are developed; includes techniques for involving nonmanagement workers in decision-making processes and for reducing reliance on hierarchical authority.

Although the plant staff had to adjust to the new style, almost everyone came to appreciate the switch to participative management because they felt as if their opinions really mattered.

See also: Authority, Communication, Decision Making, Leadership, Management, Quality Circles

Partnership

Two or more persons engaged in an enterprise; a legal association for the purpose of conducting a business.

The attorneys created a partnership when they were just out of school that lasted throughout their careers.

See also: Limited Partnership

Passive Activity

An investing activity, such as renting, in which the investor does not actively participate.

The wealthy woman chose the passive activity of renting out her properties over holding down a job in order to afford her way of life.

See also: Investing

Password

A secret combination of letters and numbers that is used to identify a user to software, network, or a computer.

The employee logged onto the company computer using her unique password.

See also: Computer, Network

Patent

An exclusive right to make, use, and sell an invention for a designated period of time; a temporary monopoly over a concept, innovation, or idea, to keep it from being stolen by imitators who suffer none of the development risk and costs.

He held out on selling his company until it was agreed his research staff could maintain the patents on everything they had created thus far.

See also: Intellectual Property

Patent Holder

One who holds or owns a patent.

The military was the patent holder for everything the captain invented while in the service.

See also: Patent

Patient

Possessing the ability to wait calmly without feeling annoyed, angry, anxious, or otherwise discontented; able to restrain from reacting rashly or ill-temperedly; not given to hurried or rash actions.

Even though she was used to micromanaging, the new team leader learned to be patient and wait for the weekly reports.

See also: Leadership

Pay for Performance

A strategy that encourages participants to think like, act like, and be paid like owners. Features a performance management/reward system in which compensation is closely tied to job performance.

Once the hotel moved to a pay-for-performance style, customer service went up throughout the entire staff.

See also: Compensation, Performance, Rewards

Payable

An amount owed.

The billing coordinator processed the payables and sent out the checks.

See also: Accounts Payable, Supplier, Vendor

Paycheck

The monetary means by which an employee is compensated for work performed, usually issued either weekly, biweekly, or monthly.

He chose to have his investments and insurance payments taken directly from his paycheck because he knew he would simply spend it all if the total amount went into his account.

See also: Compensation, Employee, Period

Payment in Kind

An exchange of value for an agreed-upon equal value.

Since the woman developed the Web page for her friend and he did her taxes, they agreed that the exchange of services was payment in kind.

See also: Agreement, Payments, Value

Payments

Agreed-upon monetary exchanges in return for goods or services.

Even during months when other bills were paid late, the cab driver made his car insurance payments on time.

See also: Cash, Disbursement, Period

Payout

The amount of money that must be raised from an advertising campaign to pay for the campaign itself.

The ad campaign was so successful that the company received its payout within the first week the commercials were on the air.

See also: Advertising, Budget, Campaign

Payroll

An employer's list of all the employees who have earned wages or salaries over a certain period of time and the amount due to each one.

The accounting department processes the payroll on the first and the fifteenth of each month.

See also: Employee, Period, Salary, Wage

Payroll Deductions

Sums withheld from an employee's gross pay to cover required and elected obligations.

She limited her payroll deductions because they were planning on having a baby and needed the extra cash.

See also: Deduction, Employee, Payroll

Peer Review

A review of work done by one audit firm or CPA by another audit firm.
As a new CPA, he was nervous about facing his first peer review.
See also: Certified Public Accountant (CPA)

Penetration Pricing

A marketing strategy in which the price is set low in order to penetrate the market quickly, maximize current revenue, increase brand share, or simply survive.
The new airline practiced penetration pricing the first year in order to build a name for itself in the highly competitive market.
See also: Brand

Pension

A sum of money paid regularly by an employer to an employee (or his dependents) once the person has retired and is eligible for such benefits.
A retiree's pension is more important than ever now that the fate of Social Security unknown.
See also: Benefits, Compensation, Deferred Compensation, Pension Fund, Retirement

Pension Fund

An account which has been set up for retired employees; funds that have been allocated to help meet the obligation of a company's retirement plan.
Many companies use the pension fund as a selling point to potential employees.
See also: Benefits, Compensation, Employee, Pension, Pension Plan, Retirement

Pension Plan

A plan for deferred compensation at retirement; a contract whereby an employer agrees to provide benefits to its employees when they retire.
The new pension plan was approved by the board of directors at the first meeting of the year.
See also: Benefits, Compensation, Defined Benefit Pension, Pension

Pent-Up Demand

Suppressed market demand for products or services; a need that is waiting to be fulfilled.
The company recognized the pent-up demand for the product and was able to capitalize on that by being first in the market.
See also: Demand, Economics, Inhibit, Supply, Suppress

Per Capita

A calculation of a number that applies equally to an individual in a population; the average amount of income per person in a population, regardless of age or labor force status.

Per capita income varies widely state by state.

See also: Income, Market Research

Per Diem

Payment by the day; or expenses paid by the day.

The shelter had several employees who worked on a per diem basis simply to cover shifts when regular staff was out.

or

The pilot was given a large per diem to cover his expenses every day he was away from home.

See also: Expenses, Payments

Per Se

Inherently; by itself; without consideration of extraneous factors.

The investor wasn't a billionaire per se but she was definitely wealthy.

See also: Intrinsic Value

Performance

Any recognized accomplishment; a process or manner of functioning or operating; management execution.

Human resources made it clear that poor performance would be penalized but that strong ones would be rewarded.

See also: Accomplishment, Execution, Management Effectiveness, Operations

Performance Bond

A bond put up by a contractor to a local government that guarantees that the work will meet the specifications and schedule.

The IT company issued a performance bond to the school district for the first six months' worth of billing.

See also: Bond, Letter of Credit

Performance Review

A way of rating or scoring employees; an appraisal instrument used to analyze the actions of an individual while on the job.

When the young man read his performance review, he was pleased to see he had been marked highly in every category.

See also: Appraisal, Communication, Employee

Period
An regular interval of time, such as a month, quarter, or year.

Analysts were cautiously optimistic the recession was ending when consumer spending rose slowly but consistently over the one-year period.

See also: Fiscal Year, Time Value of Money, Year-to-date

Peripherals
Devices that enhance a computer system.

Although many computers are affordable, adding peripherals can increase the cost dramatically.

See also: Computer, System

Perpetuity
Forever.

The founder's will specified that a place on the board should be held by a member of his family in perpetuity.

See also: Contract, Period

Perquisite or Perk
Fringe benefit that an employee gets for his time and energy; incidental benefit or right; exclusive right.

Limo service to the airport is one of the perks of the job.

See also: Benefit, Employee

Personal Digital Assistant (PDA)
One of a class of small, highly portable computers that allows a person to do a number of business functions anywhere and any time, including store names and addresses, prepare to-do lists, schedule appointments, keep track of projects, track expenditures, take notes, and do calculations; combines computing, telephone/fax, and networking features. Can also have cell phone, fax sender and personal organizer features.

Many business people have their PDAs with them at all times, even on vacation and weekends.

See also: Communication, Computer, Productivity

Perspective
A person's point of view; the choice of a context for opinions, beliefs, and experiences.

From the woman's perspective, it had been sexual harassment even though from the man's point of view he had only been joking.

See also: Belief

Persuasion
A successful attempt at changing an opinion, resulting in action.

A successful sales person needs to have excellent powers of persuasion.

See also: Change, Leadership

Persuasive
Able to convince/move/influence others; able, through the use of reason or by urging, to cause one to adopt a position, accept a belief, or take an action.

The salesman was at his most persuasive when he knew he was dealing with people looking to spend large amounts of money.

See also: Assertive, Followership, Leadership, Persuasion

PEST Analysis
An acronym that stands for the political, economic, social, and technological issues that could affect the strategic development of a business.

PEST analysis is concerned with the environmental influences on a business.

See also: Competitive Conditions, Competitive Landscape, Macroenvironmental Factors

Peter Principle
The theory that all people rise to their level of incompetence. Employees within an organization will advance to their highest level of competence and then be promoted to, and remain at, a level at which they are incompetent.

The stalling of his career wasn't about his boss not liking him but simply the Peter principle in action.

See also: Competencies, Employee, Incompetence, Organizations

Petty Cash
A small fund of cash available to staff to pay incidental expenses.

The office kept petty cash on hand to pay for incidentals and a monthly staff luncheon.

See also: Cash, Expenses

Pie Chart
A graphic in which a circle represents a whole unit, with wedges of the circle representing parts of the whole.

The sales rep broke the area population down in the pie chart in order to make it clear to his supervisor.

See also: Business Plan

Pink Slip

A termination notice.

The entire department was given pink slips because of the budget cutbacks.

See also: Employee, Termination

Pipeline

A means to the end user; various methods of bringing a product or service from the producer to the ultimate consumer using a distribution channel.

The winery owners knew that once the equipment was up and running, there would be an excellent product in the pipeline.

See also: Distribution, End User, Supply Chain, Value Chain

Planning

A management process of thinking about the activities required to create a desired future on some scale. The output of the process is a means to achieve the goal or project.

The system worked so smoothly that few people realized the long hours of planning that went into making it such a success.

See also: Balanced Scorecard, Business Plan, Communications Planning, Project, Strategic Planning

Point-of-Purchase (POP)/Point-of-Sale (POS)

Advertising and promotion at the location where the consumer actually purchases the products. May include displays strategically placed to stimulate impulse buying, usually near a check-out counter.

Even shoppers who stick rigorously to their lists when in the main store can fall prey to a well-organized POP/POS display.

See also: Advertising, Sales

Portal

A Web site that serves as a gateway or doorway to the rest of the Internet and that provides links to content on a wide variety of subjects.

An effective portal can run not only on computers but on many forms of PDAs as well.

See also: Collaboration, Extranet, Gateway, Group Discussion, Internet, Link, Search Engine, Spam, User Groups, Vortal

Porter's Five-Force Model

A model that identifies and analyzes five competitive forces that shape every industry and helps determine an industry's weaknesses and strengths. These five forces are: 1) Competition in the industry. 2) Potential of new entrants into industry. 3) Power of suppliers. 4) Power of customers. 5) Threat of substitute products.

The consultant recommended the entrepreneurs use Porter's Five-Force Model to identify which companies their new business would truly be competing with.

See also: Competition, Competitive Advantage, New Entrants, Substitute

Positioning

Determining the location of a brand or product in consumers' minds relative to competitive products; creating an image or identity in the minds of their target market for its product, brand, or organization. Developing an image for a product or service that differentiates it from its competition.

Most ad campaigns are geared toward positioning specific products over their competitors' as solutions to a consumer's needs, wants, or problems.

See also: Differentiation, Target Market

Positive

Tending to accept rather than reject, approve rather than disapprove, agree rather than disagree, and promote rather than impede.

His positive attitude during the crisis drew the attention and admiration of the management team.

See also: Motivation, Self-Confident

Power of Attorney

A legal document that authorizes one person to act as an agent for another; written authorization that lets one person act as an agent for and make binding decisions for another.

The photographer gave his accountant a power of attorney to negotiate his taxes with the IRS.

See also: Agent, Authorization, Decision Making

P

Practical

Realistic and pragmatic; useful; having to do with actual practice rather than theory.

The team was cautious about setting a practical goal for the fundraising event since it was the first time the organization had tried anything like it.

See also: Candid, Logical

Predatory Pricing

Selling products and services at a loss for a time in order to force smaller competitors out of business; an attempt to restrain trade by underselling rivals in order to acquire or preserve market share.

The airline used predatory pricing between some of its hubs during peak travel times in order to compete with the low-fare airlines.

See also: Antitrust, Entry Barriers, Market Share, Marketing

Predictive Metrics

Using metrics and measurements to predict future results by directly relating performance to an end-user's tasks.

The analysts requested predictive metrics in order to make their reports as accurate as possible.

See also: Management Information Systems (MIS), Measurements, Metrics

Preferences

Choices made from a personal perspective; a means of customizing software applications.

Many industries, from car manufacturers to computer designers, now allow customers to have their personal preferences installed at the time of purchase.

See also: Application, Market Research, Marketing, Menu, Software

Preferred Stock

A class of stock with a liquidation and dividend preference before payment is made to the common stockholders. Preferred stock is the security most used by venture capital investors.

The treasurer argued against selling the preferred stock even when the corporation needed to liquidate some assets.

See also: Stock, Stockholder or Shareholder, Venture Capital

Presentation Graphics

Software that facilitates communications in a group format using slides and other visual aids; charts, graphs, and diagrams that convey often complex business processes and outcomes to team members and clients.

Designing and preparing for his presentations became much easier once he was able to install presentation graphics on his laptop.

See also: Animation, Handout, Presentation Slides, Visual Aid

Presentation Slides

A means to communicate information and data to a group using a combination of text, graphics, and images; slides may be printed as handouts for use by the participants.

Effective speakers may use presentation slides to enhance the presentation but will do more than simply read them aloud.

See also: Bullet Points, Communications, Flipchart, Presentation Graphics, Storyboarding, Visual Aid

Price

Money paid for a product or service; what balances supply and demand.

Many consumers are willing to go from store to store in order to find the lowest price on an item.

See also: Demand, Economics, Goods, Marketing, Microeconomics, Transfer Price

Price/Earnings Ratio (P/E)

A valuation ratio used by investors to compare value among firms. The price of a share of stock divided by its earnings per share. Compares the current cost to buy shares of stock with the company's performance in the form of earnings.

The positive forecast resulted in an impressive P/E ratio for the company.

See also: Valuation

Prime Rate

The most favorable interest rate, charged to businesses that have the highest credit rating, for short term borrowing. Also the base rate at which banks charge an interest on loans to their most favored customers.

Their loan terms were prime rate plus 3 percent, and they were happy to get the funds.

See also: Credit Rating, Interest, Interest Rate

Principled
Greatly committed to one's own personal values; a person with this characteristic follows a rigorous code of conduct/ethics and has high standards.

The principled attorney volunteered at the legal center in downtown three nights a week even though she could have made more money spending those hours at the firm.

See also: Character, Convictions, Ethics, Integrity

Private Equity
An umbrella term for investments that include venture capital and buyout funds. Money that comes from wealthy individuals, pension funds, mutual funds, and investment companies such as hedge funds.

The experienced broker exclusively handled private equity funds.

See also: Venture Capital

Private Placement Memorandum (PPM)
A formal request for investment in a venture exempt from registration and filing requirements.

The investors insisted on seeing a PPM before even discussing the possibility of buying into the company.

See also: Equity Financing, Growth Capital, Offering Memorandum, Private Equity, Private Placement

Pro Forma
An indication of how management projects the future in financial terms to create a yardstick for measuring actual performance or valuing the business.

According to the pro forma, the investors could expect to see real benefits from the merger within the next fiscal year.

See also: Business Plan, Forecast

Proactive Merchandising
The use of science-based procedures including forecasting tools and techniques to optimize financial and assortment planning, buying, allocation and replenishment, and pricing and optimization.

The organization became more successful once it switched to proactive merchandising.

See also: Collaborate, Marketing, Optimization, Planning, Sales

P

Problem Solving
The process of implementing mechanisms to resolve conflicts, overcome obstacles, and improve effectiveness.

The project was far enough behind schedule that the manager called a problem-solving meeting to address the issue.

See also: Conflict Resolution, Obstacles, Problem Taking

Problem Taking
A knack for picking and choosing the right problems for an organization to tackle; a better path through the marketplace forest. It is more than a brilliant strategy; it is the ability to continuously select the right path in an ever-changing terrain.

She was hired by the floundering organization because of her reputation for having excellent problem-taking skills.

See also: Organizations, Problem Solving

Problems
Specific tasks or questions to be considered, solved, or answered, rising to importance as a result of unsatisfactory performance, barriers to obtaining a goal, or environmental changes.

The team knew once the problems were identified, they could be dealt with and the project could move forward.

See also: Barriers, Goals, Obstacles, Problem Solving, Problem Taking, Task

Process
A systematic method of obtaining a desired result; a series of actions, changes, or functions with inputs, method, and outputs; a collection of related structural activities that produces something of value to the organization, its stakeholders, or its customers.

The new director was wise enough to earn her staff's trust before instituting new changes to the process that had been in place for so long.

See also: Organization, Results, Stakeholders

Product
Anything that can be offered to the marketplace; a measurable entity created as a result of a process or project; something that is deliverable with a benefit to the user or consumer.

Part of becoming a success in business is to offer the right product at the right time.

See also: Product Development, Product Marketing

Product Development

A strategy in which products are developed to meet the needs of existing customers. Product innovation is driven by the market demand for the firm's current offerings and may require new competencies or new perspectives.

Although the company had been wildly successful, they continued to grow because they were willing to put money into product development.

See also: Benefits, Creative, Innovation, Prototype

Product Differentiation

The process of providing products that are distinctly different from those of competitors; usually based on research on specific customer wants and needs.

Attempts to achieve product differentiation have resulted in some very interesting soft-drink flavors.

See also: Competitive Advantage, Position, Strategy

Product Liability

The responsibility of the manufacturer, wholesaler, or retailer for damages occurring through use of a product. Product liability is the area of law in which firms who make products available to the public are held responsible for injuries those products cause.

Product liability can be reduced to an extent by the addition of warning labels.

See also: Responsibility

Product Life Cycle

The phases required to develop an item intended for the marketplace; the succession of stages that item goes through before it is ready to be sold.

The company took pride in the fact that their product life cycle was shorter than their competitors' and the end product was of better quality.

See also: Life Cycle, Product Development, Product Life Cycle Management (PLM), Time-to-Market

Product Life Cycle Management (PLM)

A business strategy that helps companies manage the succession of stages a product goes through by sharing product data, applying common processes, and leveraging corporate knowledge for the development of products from conception to retirement, across the extended enterprise.

Product life cycle management gave the team a big-picture understanding of the venture, which made it more successful in the long run.

See also: Life Cycle, Management, Product, Strategy

Product Marketing

Developing a demand for a product or service; establishing a product brand in the marketplace; creating competitive advantage for a product.

Product marketing can be the difference between a successful venture and one that barely registers in the industry.

See also: Brand, Competitive Advantage, Marketing

Product Mix

The combination of offerings a firm provides to its customers and clients. A product mix can be either wide/broad (offering a large number of products) or narrow/limited (offering only a few products).

The singer had a broad enough product mix that she was able to tailor her song choices to each specific audience depending on the situation and venue.

See also: Marketing, Product

Product Obsolescence

The diminishing of a product's usefulness and attraction, usually due to the introduction of new and improved items that perform better, are less expensive, or both.

Just as MP3 players have made portable CD players seem archaic, one day some new product will send MP3 players into product obsolescence.

See also: Market, Near-Term Market, Obsolescence, Opportunities, Technical Obsolescence

Production

The means or methods of creating products that add value to the economy; or a presentation or event.

The production time for the new project turned out to be much longer than originally estimated.

or

What was supposed to be a small presentation turned into a production when many others on the staff requested they be allowed to sit in.

See also: Manufacturing, Presentation

Production Capacity

The volume of products or services that can be created by an enterprise using current resources.

The bottling line was the limitation on the facility's production capacity.

See also: Capacity, Production, Productivity, Resources

Productive

With a high work output; characterized by the ability to accomplish a great deal of work without wasting time or energy.

The team was so productive that it led the department in sales almost every quarter.

See also: Efficiency

Productivity

A measure of efficiency, sometimes expressed as a ratio of output to input.

Whenever the plant's productivity dropped, the mechanics were called in to overhaul and tune up the equipment.

See also: Efficiency, Productive

Professional

Having the specialized knowledge or training necessary to carry out the activities of a vocation; able to carry out the activities of a vocation effectively and efficiently; having an understanding of, and acting in accordance with, the principles of conduct or the work standards of a vocation.

Although he had often helped his friends with projects around the house, he never considered becoming a professional carpenter.

See also: Accomplished, Career

Profit

What results from revenues when all expenses have been paid; reward for risk taken by the organization and the leadership.

Since most stores don't turn a profit during the first few years, a second source of income is often necessary.

See also: Income Statement, Loss

Profit and Loss (P&L) Statement

A report on the performance of an enterprise in a specific time period. A financial statement that shows an organization's revenues, expenses, and net income for a particular period. This report is also called an income statement or earnings statement.

The treasurer paid closer attention to the P&L statement as the economic forecast started to concern her.

See also: Financial Statement or Reports, Income Statement

Profit Margin

A measure of profitability; the percentage of each dollar of sales that is net income; net income divided by sales.

She knew the salon's profit margin would have to increase in the next quarter if she was going to be able to stay in business.

See also: Asset Turnover, Financial Ratios, Profit

Profit Potential

The amount of money that can be made from a venture.

Even if the profit potential for a new business is high, one should consider the challenges of starting a new venture before simply jumping in.

See also: Forecast, Profit, Venture

Profit Sharing

An incentive program for employees in which a company distributes a portion of its profits to employees.

The airline's customer service increased noticeably when the CEO instituted profit sharing within the company.

See also: Compensation, Profit

Program

A group of related projects that are managed together; means for an organization or group of organizations to achieve stated goals; system of projects or services intended to meet a business or public need; a sequence of instructions that a computer can interpret and execute.

The clinic was one of several programs the nonprofit ran out of the old hospital.

See also: Project

Program Evaluation and Review Techniques (PERT)

A method for analyzing the tasks involved in completing a given project, especially the time needed to complete each task, and identifying the minimum time needed to complete the total project.

The program director always appreciated being presented with a PERT network diagram at the beginning of a new project even if she wasn't going to be directly involved.

See also: Bar Chart, Critical Path, Gantt Chart, Project Management, Work Breakdown Structure (WBS)

Program Management

The process of managing a portfolio of multiple ongoing interdependent projects.

He was given the promotion to oversee the department largely because of his program management skills.

See also: Coordination, Project Management, Resource Allocation

Project

A planned undertaking; a group of tasks aimed toward a common objective with a finite start and finish.

A subcommittee was formed to assess the feasibility of the project and report back to the whole board.

See also: Objectives, Planning, Project Management, Task

Project Life Cycle

The management phases of a project, including initiation and scope definition; planning; execution, control and coordination; and closure, acceptance, and support.

Proper planning and coordination can eliminate many glitches during the project life cycle of a new scheme.

See also: Life Cycle, Project, Project Management

Project Management

The discipline, knowledge, skills, and techniques of planning, organizing, controlling, and managing resources in such a way that these resources deliver all the work required to complete a project within defined scope, time, and cost constraints.

The team leader excelled in program management so supervisors were never concerned about his workload.

See also: Critical Path, Program Evaluation and Review Techniques (PERT), Project, Resources

Project Manager

The person responsible for providing leadership to a team and managing the project and its associated work to ensure that expected results are obtained.

The project manager was excited about finally being given responsibility and the opportunity to prove himself.

See also: Leadership, Project Management, Resource Allocation

Projectized Organization

An organizational structure that is focused on projects. The project manager has authority over the resources assigned to the project.

The new Airbus is being developed using a projectized organization.

See also: Matrix Organization, Organizational Structure, Project Manager

Promotion

A marketing strategy to improve brand and profitability and to stimulate demand for a product. Forms of communication that call attention to products and services, typically by adding extra value to the purchase. Includes temporary discounts, allowances, premium offers, coupons, contests, and rebates.

The director's last movie had been such a disappointment that the studio scaled back the promotion for his next one.

See also: Advertising, Brand, Communication, Marketing, Product

Promotional Materials

Materials used to market and sell products and services, such as advertising literature, brochures, flyers, sales literature, newsletters, and mailers.

The club hired people to pass out promotional materials and to paper the neighborhood with the announcement of the popular DJ's appearance.

See also: Advertising, Marketing, Sales

Proof of Concept

A project or phase in which a team attempts to prove through some form of demonstration whether a concept, activity, or an idea can be accomplished.

The team knew the idea was a good one and hoped their proof of concept presentation would convince the managers as well.

See also: Project

Proprietary/Proprietary Rights

Intellectual property is owned by the enterprise, such as a patent, formula, brand name, or trademark associated with the product/service.

Musicians tend to be very protective of the proprietary rights attached to their work.

See also: Brand, Patent, Trademark

Proprietary Technology

Technology that is unique and legally owned by an enterprise, usually protected as intellectual property. The technology may be intrinsic to the product or service being offered or it may be used in the production of the product or service.

Few people realize that client names and marketing strategies can fall under the umbrella of proprietary technology just as formulas and other trade secrets do.

See also: Nondisclosure Agreement (NDA), Technology

Proprietorship

A common legal form of business in which the business owner is the proprietor. All the legal liability resides with the owner, who is entitled to all profits as well as liabilities and losses. The most common legal form of business ownership; about 85 percent of all small businesses are proprietorships.

The brothers entered into joint proprietorship so they would share everything as equals.

See also: Profit, Sole Proprietorship, Structure, Taxes

Prospect

A prospective customer or client who has the means and capacity to buy a product or service, but a decision to do so is pending; a qualified lead. Also referred to as a potential customer.

The owners of the winery met several new prospects at the gourmet auction.

See also: Campaign, Client, Customer, Sales

Prospecting

A process by which marketing and salespeople determine whether or not a business or an individual might qualify as a potential customer.

Accurate prospecting is a challenge because one must not make assumptions based on first impressions.

See also: Campaign, Lead, Prospect, Sales

Prospectus

A formal written offer to sell equity in a company or enterprise. It gives a plan for the proposed business enterprise or the facts concerning an existing business that an investor needs to make an informed investment decision.

The broker read each prospectus carefully before advising her clients about any one company.

See also: Equity, Investment, Offering Memorandum

Prototype

An original, full-scale, and usually working model of a new product, innovation, or new version of an existing product.

Many car manufacturers will unveil a prototype at a trade show in order to gauge the public's reaction before sending the model to the assembly line.

See also: Innovation, Product Development

Proxy

A right given to an agent or other designated party, most often in the context of shareholder-voting in corporations. Or a document sent by public companies to their shareholders providing information on company matters subject to vote at the company's annual meeting.

Since she was going to be out of the country at the time of the vote, she made arrangements for her brother to vote in proxy for her.

or

The young man had so few shares in the company that he generally threw away the proxy without even a glance when it arrived in the mail.

See also: Corporation

Public Accounting

The field of accounting that offers services in auditing, taxation, and management advising to the public for a fee. Such accountants are certified and are referred to as certified public accountants (CPAs).

Many people who enjoy working with numbers and finances choose public accounting as a career.

See also: Accounting, Audit, Certified Public Accountant (CPA)

Public Company

A company whose shares are sold to the public at large in accordance with Securities and Exchange Commission (SEC) regulations.

The woman's business broke sales records the day it became a public company.

See also: Corporation, Equity, Stockholder or Shareholder

Public Domain

A copyright term that describes a collection of works that are free for all to use without permission. Works in the public domain include those that were never copyrighted, those for which the copyright has expired, and public documents.

The Internet and easily accessible information has created great debate about what is in the public domain and what is not.

See also: Copyright, Disclosure

Public Offering

The sale of a company's shares of stock to the public by a company or its major stockholders.

The announcement of a public offering from the notoriously tight-fisted company had brokers' phones ringing off their hooks.

See also: Initial Public Offering (IPO), Public Company, Stock, Stockholder or Shareholder

Public Relations

Communication geared to increase public awareness and/or opinion, create a brand, and effect acceptance of a company, person, product, or idea using a variety of skills and tactics developed to create favorable opinion for a person, event, or product that ultimately supports the firm's bottom line.

Since the product was tested on animals, good public relations were essential to keep customers happy.

See also: Brand, Communication, Marketing

Publicity

Media information that is used to create a brand or promote a product, service, or idea.

The movie's stars went on a publicity tour to create interest in the small-budget film.

See also: Brand, Communication, Public Relations

Publicly Held Corporation

A corporation registered with the Securities and Exchange Commission (SEC) and whose securities are traded on the open market, available to anyone.

As a publicly held corporation, its stocks were available to purchase online or through brokerage companies.

See also: Equity, Public Company, Security, Stock, Stockholder or Shareholder

Pull Promotional Strategy

A marketing strategy that requires direct interface with the end user. Production and distribution are demand driven so that they are coordinated with true customer demand rather than forecast demand.

The tech firm used a pull promotional strategy to build its customer base and differentiate itself from mass-market firms within the industry.

See also: Direct Marketing, End User

Punctual

Consistently on time. A person with this characteristic pays strict attention to the schedule and performs all tasks on time.

The CEO expected people attending meetings to respect each others' busy schedules by being punctual and ready to work.

See also: Reliable, Response, Time Management

Purchase Order (PO)

A form, document, or electronic communication that contains pricing, quantity, unique tracking number, and other purchasing information.

Some shopping companies will issue a purchase order to help ensure the right package gets to the right customer.

See also: Supplier

Purchase Price

The amount a consumer pays for a product or service.

She loved outlet stores because the purchase price on items was so much lower than retail.

See also: Consumer, Price

Purchasing Accounting

An accounting methodology that treats an acquisition as an investment. Assets are added to the purchasing company's balance sheet. If the purchase price is above the market value, the difference is recorded as goodwill and must be charged again in future earnings.

Using purchasing accounting, the target company was an excellent investment for the smaller firm because of the goodwill it brought to the table.

See also: Accounting, Assets, Balance Sheet, Goodwill, Merger

Purpose

The "why" and "how" behind an organization's existence; the aim or goals toward which an organization strives or for which it exists. The statement defining how the constituent's or stakeholder's interests are balanced; the incorporation of management's values.

The purpose of the organization was to ensure all people received sound legal advice regardless of income or ability to pay.

See also: Mission, Roles, Stakeholder, Values, Vision

Push Promotional Strategy

A marketing strategy to maximize the use of all available channels of distribution to send the product or service into the marketplace in the hopes of creating demand products that are "pushed" through the channel, from the production side up to the retailer.

He was a good sale rep because of his ability to use push promotional strategy well enough to get the dog food into the major national pet store chains.

See also: Distribution, Marketing Strategy, Retailer

Q

Quality

The degree to which the product or project meets or exceeds requirements.

The quality of the jelly depended almost entirely on how fresh the produce was when it arrived at the plant.

See also: Continuous Improvement, Quality Circles, Six Sigma, Total Quality Management (TQM)

> **Quality** is difficult to define. It's an abstract measure that requires continuous and dynamic adaptation of products and services if they are to fulfill or exceed the requirements or expectations of all parties in the organization and the community as a whole. Although explaining what **quality** is may be difficult, recognizing what it is not tends to be much easier.

Quality Assurance

A system to ensure a management process for quality in products and services; a means of preventing defects; a refined process in which products are assessed, improved, ensured, and confirmed to achieve excellence in a product/service by meeting/exceeding the requirements of the customer.

The quality assurance team worked overtime to ensure the new software couldn't crash easily.

See also: Kaizen, Quality, Quality Control, Six Sigma, Statistical Control

Quality Circle

A team or group that improves the quality of a process, product, or service through communications and experimentation.

The quality circle met once a month to address issues ranging from better snacks in the vending machines to the inequality of the treatment given parents within the organization.

See also: Continuous Improvement, Kaizen, Quality, Teams, Total Quality Management (TQM)

Quality Control

A management process to improve the quality of products and services; a way to ensure that products or services are designed and produced to meet or exceed customer requirements and expectations.

Once the baker hired assistants and was no longer the only one in the kitchen, he became even more vigilant about quality control.

See also: Pareto Chart, Quality, Six Sigma, Total Quality Management (TQM)

Quality Expectations

The standards used to measure the quality of a product within a specific tier or segment.

The goal of the new CEO was to raise the company's quality expectations enough to make the company a major player among Wall Street firms.

See also: Quality

Quality Oriented

A team or team member who shows unfailing commitment to quality; motivated to achieve superior results; interested in and appreciative of excellence.

As a quality-oriented manager, she was more hands-on than supervisors the staff had worked with in the past.

See also: Excellence, Motivation

Quantity Discount

A favorable price cut given in exchange for purchasing or buying in volume.

The technology firm offered a quantity discount of 5 percent on all orders larger than 1,000 units.

See also: Discount Rate

Quarterly Report

Financial report published every three months containing information about
a company's fiscal status.

*Quarterly reports are read carefully by people who want to track the financial
stability of a company, such as fund managers.*

See also: 10Q, Financial Statement or Reports, Stockholder or Shareholder

Questioning

Requesting information; interpersonal communication leading to discovery and invention. A means to sell or buy-in to a project, product, or program. Closed questions are those that elicit yes/no answers. Open questions are those that elicit longer responses. Personal questions have a special role in leadership and can create a sense of camaraderie between employee and boss.

*Often he found himself questioning his mentors and colleagues on minor and
major points, based on his own firsthand observations and research.*

See also: Communication, Listening

Quick Assets

The sum of marketable securities, receivables, and cash; assets that can be
quickly liquidated. Quick assets are also defined as current assets minus
inventory.

*When they needed to increase the firm's liquidity, the management team
requested a listing of the quick assets currently available.*

See also: Accounts Receivables, Assets, Cash, Liquid, Security

Quick Ratio

A metric that measures a firm's liquidity or its ability to pay off liabilities
quickly with the funds that are currently available. This ratio is calculated by
taking the quick assets (current assets minus inventory) divided by current
liabilities. This ratio is also referred to as the acid-test ratio.

*The CFO preferred to keep the corporation's quick ratio reasonable even though
he trusted they would never have to pay off their debts that fast.*

See also: Current Assets, Current Liabilities, Financial Ratios, Inventories

Quick-Thinking

Characterized by rapid powers of comprehension; able to exercise one's mental powers rapidly, particularly one's powers of reason.

*The quick-thinking attorney won several cases simply because she could react
well in the court room.*

See also: Crisis, Decision Making, Responsive

Quiet Period

The period that extends from the time an agreement to sell stock is reached until ninety days after the transaction is completed, during which the Securities and Exchange Commission (SEC) prohibits an issuer from speaking publicly about the business. There are serious penalties for noncompliance.

The management team went on the road to sell their stock to investors as soon as their quiet period passed.

See also: Initial Public Offering (IPO), Public Offering

R

Rate of Return

A metric for economic success; the gain or loss of an investment over a specified period, expressed as a percentage increase over the initial investment cost. A rate of return measurement can be used to measure virtually any investment or project.

A positive rate of return is a good indication that this project would be a good investment.

See also: Discount Rate, Discounted Cash Flow, Internal Rate of Return (IRR), Net Present Value (NPV), Time Value of Money

Ratio Analysis

A tool for a firm to compare its performance with that of other firms in the same industry. Compares results from historical performance; used to develop metrics for teams, projects, or individuals.

The board requested a ratio analysis hoping to understand why the firm was suddenly struggling.

See also: Benchmark, Financial Ratios

Rationalization

Systematic organization; organization of a business according to scientific principles of management in order to increase efficiency; practical application of knowledge to achieve a desired end.

When faced with the crisis, the board realized everything about the organization needed to change, from overhead costs and portfolio rationalization to the morale of the staff.

See also: Change Management, Organization

Raw Materials
The unprocessed materials used to produce an item or create a work in process. The production process results in a change of form from the original materials. Reported on the balance sheet as inventory when unused.

It is amazing to watch the load of raw materials that arrive at the plant being turned into such an elegant and sophisticated product.

See also: Balance Sheet, Inventories, Work-in-process

Receipt
A statement showing that goods, services, money or another item of value has been received; may be physical, written, or electronic.

He showed his receipt to the security guard to prove he hadn't stolen the DVD.

See also: Acquittance, Cash Basis Accounting, Invoice, Statement

Recruiting
The process of seeking out qualified candidates to fill openings within a company.

At the end of every school year, firms will send representatives to campuses for the purpose of recruiting new hires.

See also: Hiring, Human Resource Management, Labor Pool

Recycle
To use again after processing; to remanufacture old systems, products, and equipment.

One of the challenges of the computer age was figuring out how to recycle old computer parts so they didn't just get dumped in landfills.

See also: Product Life Cycle, Remanufacturing

Red Herring
A preliminary prospectus, distributed to prospective investors, with a legend in red ink on the cover stating that (SEC approval) registration statement has yet to be obtained.

The red herring drew the attention of several prospective investors, which then increased the buzz around the upcoming offering.

See also: Prospectus, Registration

Red Ink
A descriptive term indicating that a venture or enterprise is losing money.

The venture capital firm funded six businesses last year and five are still in red ink this year.

See also: Cash Flow, Loss, Venture Capital

Redundancy

Duplication exceeding what is necessary or normal; several different methods capable of performing the same task.

The redundancy of the two positions demanded that one of them be eliminated in order to save the costs of having both employees on staff.

See also: Quality, Repetition

Reengineering

The fundamental reconsideration and radical redesign of organizational processes in order to achieve drastic improvement of current performance in cost, service, and speed; a systematic, disciplined improvement approach that critically examines, rethinks, redesigns, and implements the redesigned mission-delivery processes in areas important to customers and other stakeholders.

In order to move into the twenty-first century, the company needed to be reengineered at just about every level.

See also: Change Management, Organizations, Stakeholders, Teams

Referral

The act of directing someone or something to another source; someone who is directed to another source for help or information; a client who is transferred from one professional to another.

Before hiring any company to perform a major task, it is wise to ask for referrals from other customers.

See also: Communication, Relationship

Refinance

A process of renewing, revising, or reorganizing existing debt that incorporates or pays off current debt.

The couple decided to refinance their house in order to pay off their credit cards and lower their monthly bills.

See also: Debt, Reorganize

Registered Stock or Security

Stock that has been registered with the Securities and Exchange Commission (SEC) and thus can be sold publicly.

The fact that there was a limited amount of registered stock available for purchase increased demand even more.

See also: Publicly Held, Registration, Registration Statement, Stock

Registration Statement

The document that details the purpose of a public offering, filed with the Securities and Exchange Commission (SEC).

In preparation for the initial public offering, the firm delivered its registration statement to the SEC.

See also: Public Offering, Registered Company, Registered Stock or Security

Regulated Company

A company whose marketplace is subject to governmental limitations, legislation, or rules under federal or state laws.

As part of a regulated company, the oil rig workers had to be mindful of environmental damage.

See also: Federal Laws, Legislation

Relationship

The way in which two or more organizations, concepts, objects, or people are connected, or the state of being connected.

The owners of the winery went to the trade show in order to build relationships with nationwide distributors.

See also: Client, Collaborate, Customer, Network, Relationship Marketing

Relationship Marketing

A marketing strategy that places an emphasis on building longer-term relationships with customers rather than on individual transactions; involves the understanding, focusing, and management of ongoing collaboration between suppliers and selected customers for mutual value and creation.

The auto industry relies heavily on relationship marketing, hoping that families and even successive generations will stay with one make of car.

See also: Collaboration, Customer, Marketing Strategy, Relationship

Reliable

Dependable and constant; able to be counted on.

We hired the interns to be full-time employees because they proved reliable.

See also: Accurate, Consistent, Stable

Remanufacturing

Manufacturing an old, worn-out product into a new and usable product using assemblies and parts from previous systems or units.

Remanufacturing laptops results in products that are usually as dependable as new ones and that can cost hundreds of dollars less.

See also: Manufacturing, Product Life Cycle, Recycle

Request for Proposal (RFP)

An announcement inviting companies to submit plans for providing a product or service and/or bids for the price of providing it, along with schedules, technical information, and a method of management.

RFPs often include specifications of the item, project, or service for which a proposal is requested.

See also: Invitation for Bid, Request for Information, Request for Quote

Research Interview

Fact finding in order to collect new data to solve an information need using direct questioning as the means to acquire the information. A few examples include user surveys, focus groups, phone interviews and customer questionnaires.

The college student took a job conducting research interviews on the plaza in order to have more spending money.

See also: Group Interview, Interview, Market Research

Reserved

Composed, controlled, and sedate; not given to boisterous expression or showy behavior.

His reserved nature made him better with the technical end of the project than with the fundraising.

See also: Congenial, Self-confident

Resource

Anything needed to complete a project, task, or goal. May be people, information, equipment, facilities, leadership, or capital.

The project was so large that the director hired part-time workers and authorized overtime so that the team would have all the resources necessary to complete it on time.

See also: Business Planning, Goal, Resource Analysis, Resource Planning, Task

Resource Allocation

The process of distributing and assigning resources among various projects or business units; a management decision process; a means for strategy implementation.

During times of scarcity, resource allocation becomes more important but also more difficult.

See also: Decision Making, Implementation, Project, Resources, Scheduling, Slack Resources, Strategic Business Unit, Strategic Planning, Total Quality Management (TQM), Tradeoffs

Responsibility

A duty to act in a professional manner and put the interest of stakeholders first; trustworthiness in all business dealings; the act of being responsible.

As researchers, they believed they had a responsibility to the environment as well as the stockholders to find new fuel alternatives.

See also: Accountability, Authority, Leadership, Obligation, Trustworthiness, Values

Responsible

Dependable and reliable; able to be trusted to fulfill one's obligations and commitments and to conduct oneself in a dependable, trustworthy manner.

As a team member she is very responsible and can be relied on to closely examine all sides of an important business issue before making a decision.

See also: Reliable

Responsive

The quality of responding promptly and willingly; of reacting readily.

The building manager was always responsive when the IT team notified her that the air conditioning system in the computer area had failed.

See also: Quick Reaction

Results

The outcome of a process, project, or activity; the things that are measured in a business or venture.

An annual report contains details on financial results and performance of the previous fiscal year, as well as perspective for the future.

See also: Outcome, Problem Solving, Project

Retailer

A company or individual that sells commodities or goods to the ultimate consumer. Generally a retailer buys wholesale, marks up the items, and sells.

Some retailers allow teenagers to hang out around their storefronts while others do not appreciate having the door blocked.

See also: Consumer, Distribution

Retained Earnings

Net income that is kept within the organization. Income a company has earned, less the dividends it has paid. Retained earnings equal net earnings minus dividends.

Retained earnings are the amount of money that a company keeps for future use or investment.

See also: Earnings Per Share

Retainer

A fee given to a service professional for advice, services, or help.

The actress paid an attorney a retainer so she could call on him whenever necessary.

See also: Fee, Professional

Retirement

The time of life after one has quit working; one may enter retirement either voluntarily or forcibly due to age, disability, or sickness.

The couple planned on traveling the world once they reached retirement age.

See also: Career

Return on Assets (ROA)

A metric that shows a firm's ability to produce net assets; computed by dividing earnings by assets. The higher the ratio, the more effective the company is at using its assets to produce profits.

The ROA analysis showed the business had come out of the slump and was back on track financially.

See also: Financial Ratios

Return on Equity (ROE)

Measures the return on the owner's (shareholders') investment in the company; perhaps the most important measure of a business's financial viability. The higher the ratio, the higher the rate of return on a shareholder's investment. Net income divided by book value of shareholders' equity equals return on equity.

Since the company had consistent earning power and strong ROE, its board was often approached by larger companies to discuss the possibility of a merger.

See also: Book Value, Equity, Financial Ratios, Investment, Stockholder or Shareholder

Return on Investment (ROI)

A financial ratio indicating the degree of profitability. The amount of profit (return) based on the amount of resources (funds) used to produce it. Net income divided by book value of assets equals return on investment.

The investors were pleased with the ROI that the business was showing after only two years.

See also: Assets, Book Value, Financial Ratios, Profit, Resources

Revenue

The gross income received before any expenses are deducted; money collected from customers for the sale of a product or service. Increases in assets or reductions in liabilities that result in an increase in equity during a reporting period.

The firm's revenue was not high enough to pay the bills, so cuts had to be made.

See also: Clients, Customer, Gross Sales

Rewards

A means to strengthen approved behavior; payment made in return for a service rendered; recognition of team's behavior or actions.

In order to maintain group unity, the director only gave out rewards to the entire team, not individuals.

See also: Behavior, Compensation, Customer Relationship Management (CRM), Intangible Rewards, Payments, Recognition, Team

Rightsizing

The restructuring of a company, project, or organization after evaluating tasks to eliminate duplications and inefficiencies; sizing an organization to compete.

Even though his company referred to it as rightsizing, he still felt as if he had been fired.

See also: Downsizing, Layoff, Lean Organization, Organizations, Outplacement

Risk

The chance that events, things, or outcomes will turn out differently from what is expected.

Any new venture has certain risks involved, but many entrepreneurs thrive on the challenge.

See also: Risk Assessment, Risk Capital, Risk Factor

Risk Assessment

Identifying risks to a project and determining their effect.

The team's risk assessment showed the project was worthwhile to the company because damage would be minimal if it failed.

See also: Project, Risk, Risk Identification

Risk Factor

An estimate of the chance of loss with a new venture.

The risk factor in signing the temperamental artist was so high that no record label was willing to chance it.

See also: New Venture, Risk, Risk Management

Risk Identification

The process of identifying potential risks and their associated characteristics along with the positive or negative impact they may have on the enterprise, venture, or project.

A special team was assigned the task of risk identification before the firm agreed to the new project.

See also: Project, Risk, Venture

Risk Management

A process for mitigating potential risks through effective management; analyzing and managing risk to reduce the frequency, severity, or unpredictability of accidental losses.

The CEO trusted her staff to handle the risk management well enough to make the project a success.

See also: Business Plan, Management, Risk, Risk Assessment, Risk Mitigation

Risk Mitigation

The response to an unacceptable risk that lowers it to an acceptable level.

While unlikely, the chance that the database would crash under certain conditions was still high enough that the project manager required risk mitigation before allowing the product to be released to the public.

See also: Risk, Risk Factor, Risk Management

Rivalry Among Industry Competitors

The degree to which competitors producing products that are close substitutes for each other influence prices and profits in a given industry. The external and internal pressures that executives are faced with as they redeploy their assets in response to competitive pressures.

The rivalry among industry competitors in the soft-drink industry is so strong and so tight that the odds of a new brand breaking into the market are slim.

See also: Competitive Advantage, Differentiation, Exit Barriers, Porter's Five-Force Model, Strategy

Rolling Average

Continuously or periodically calculating and updating the average of a given variable to reflect new data.

The six-month rolling average sales trailed the current month's sales, so the team was happy.

See also: Financial Ratios, Metrics, Ratio Analysis

Roundtable

A group of whose members all enjoy equal status, whose job is to focus on issues it believes will have an impact on their stakeholders; serves as a catalyst in working with other groups to form coalitions and in stimulating individual business leaders to be more active in developing strategy and policy.

Since the attorneys often met as a roundtable, they had to be especially careful of conflicts of interest.

See also: Communications, Leadership, Management, Stakeholders, Strategy

Royalties

Payments for the rights to use intellectual property or natural resources.

The advertising department paid the musicians royalties for the use of the song in the commercial.

See also: Royalty Revenue

Royalty Revenue

Revenue recognized upon sale by the licensee of royalty-bearing products, as estimated by the company, and when realization is considered probable by management.

Twenty-five percent to the semiconductor firm's profits came from royalty revenue from licenses to firms in China and India.

See also: Royalties

S

S Corporation

A firm that has elected to be taxed as a partnership under the subchapter S provision of the Internal Revenue Code.

The IRS has imposed restrictions on S corporations to ensure that companies don't use that status to avoid corporate taxes.

See also: Corporation, Taxes

Salary

Regular, fixed compensation paid to an employee as a condition of employment during a specific time period.

He was willing to accept a lower salary than he'd had in previous jobs in order to take a position that allowed him to spend more time with his family.

See also: Compensation, Employee, Wage

Sales

Revenue, money, or the promise of money a company receives from providing its products and services to customers; or the process of creating and servicing customers. Reported on the company's income statement.

The company's sales always dropped off dramatically during the winter.

or

It takes a certain personality to be successful in sales, especially when cold-calling is involved.

See also: Gross Sales, Income Statement, Revenue

Sales Agent

A person who works as a subcontractor for a company and sells products/services.

She was able to supplement the family's income as a sales agent for the beauty product company.

See also: Sales

Sales and Marketing Expenses

The expenses incurred in carrying out the activities listed in the marketing section of the firm's business plan; reported on the company's income statement.

The budget included sales and marketing expenses for the distributor.

See also: Business Plan, Income Statement

Sales Draft

The electronic evidence of a purchase.

The e-commerce business sent out a sales draft via e-mail upon completion of the online transaction.

See also: Purchase Order (PO)

Sales Forecast

A projection of the anticipated sales volume of a product or service.

The product sold much better than the sales forecast led them to expect.

See also: Business Plan, Forecast, Sales

Sales Manager

A manager who oversees the planning and directing of sales efforts in his or her designated area of responsibilities. In addition, this person usually supervises one or more salespeople.

The sales manager answered directly to the owner and was often in charge of the floor when the owner was out.

See also: Sales, Sales Management

S

Sales Quota

A sales goal assigned to a sales person or team for use in the management of sales efforts; usually for some specific time period, territory, or product.

Every clerk had to meet a specific sales quota in order for the business to clear a profit.

See also: Goals, Sales Forecast

Sales Representative

A person who works as a subcontractor for a company and who represents and sells products/services; the job title of one who represents the company to the customer in a specific time period, territory, or product.

The sales representative for the dog food was able to explain what made his product more nutritious than its competitors.

See also: Sales Agent, Territory

Sales Transaction

An e-commerce payment authorization transaction that allows a merchant to authorize a transaction then capture the payment for deposit in a single electronic message to the purchaser, such as an e-mail or text message.

The online store saw its sales transactions increase thanks to the ads it was placing on other sites.

See also: E-Commerce, Sales

Satisficing

The act of settling for an acceptable level of success rather than aiming for the highest possible success. Most often occurs when decision makers within a business must achieve several separate goals simultaneously.

The designer of the program was frustrated with management's satisficing of the program because he knew it was capable of so much more than they were allowing him to produce.

See also: Decision Making, Economics

Saturation

A phase of the product life cycle in which the demand for the product has decreased rapidly. At this stage, most of the people with an interest in the product have already purchased it.

In many communities, the service industry has reached the saturation point, making it a less desirable industry than it once was for entrepreneurs.

See also: Product Development, Product Life Cycle, Product Life Cycle Management (PLM)

Scenario

An approach for exploring the future and developing strategies for thriving in new environments, making strategic choices, or dealing with market uncertainties. Executives identify surprises and discontinuities in every area of their business, from customer demand and adoption of new technologies to changing market and regulatory environments using a perspective outlook on future events and trends.

The job of the quality control engineers was to anticipate and recreate real-world scenarios and make sure the software didn't crash.

See also: Business Plan, Strategic Choices, Strategy, Uncertainty

Schedule

The timeline for a project, including start and end dates for project activities.

The release schedule for the new software was tight, but the designers were confident it could be met.

See also: Milestone

Scheduling

Planning and organizing tasks, activities, and people to be more efficient and effective.

The staff coordinator felt lucky to have enough employees that she could easily handle any scheduling conflicts.

See also: Effective, Efficiency, Resource Allocation, Time Management

Scope

Objectives, business justifications, and goals that are considered part of the enterprise, project, or task; area in which leadership acts or operates or has power or control.

The CEO's vision and scope for the plant was reinvigorated after touring similar sites in the Midwest and seeing the successes there.

See also: Control, Goals, Leadership, Objectives, Strategy

Search Engine

Software that indexes Web pages; a program designed to help find information stored on a computer system such as the World Wide Web, a corporate or proprietary network, or a personal computer.

Nearly all regular computer users have a search engine they prefer and believe to be the most comprehensive.

See also: Data Mining, Internet, Intranet, Keyword, Portal, World Wide Web (WWW)

Seasonality
The variation of sales activity caused by the time of the year.

Sales of bathing suits are subject to seasonality, selling more in the spring and summer than in the cooler months.

See also: Sales

Seconds
Merchandise, products, goods, or commodities that are slightly damaged or have previously been handled and are usually sold at discounted prices.

The warehouse store sold last year's fashions and seconds at dramatically reduced prices.

See also: Retailer

Secret Partners
An active partner whose membership in the partnership is not revealed to the public.

The actor chose to be a secret partner in the C corporation so his affiliation would not draw attention away from the organization's mission.

See also: Disclosure, Partnership

Secretary of State
The body of government in each state that regulates business registrations among other things.

Generally speaking, the right to incorporate is granted by the Secretary of State.

See also: Articles of Incorporation, Corporate Bylaws, Incorporate

Security
The process of protecting a company's assets; or a term for stocks and bonds.

Encrypting documents and requiring passwords on all computers was part of the security for the confidential databases.

or

The company founder refused to release enough securities to give anyone else a majority holding.

See also: E-Commerce, Network, Trade Secret

S

SEC Filings
Required papers concerning a company's finances and operations that are submitted to the federal Securities and Exchange Commission (SEC) as required by law.

The corporation was fined when its SEC filings were late.

See also: 10K, 10Q

Seed Capital
Initial money to get a venture going; funds from angel investors and venture capitalist in the early stages of a business.

Her stepfather loaned her the seed money with the understanding it would be paid back within the first two years the business was profitable.

See also: Angels, First-Round Financing, Front Money, Seed Stage, Venture Capital, Venture Capitalists

Seed Stage
The initial stage of a venture; describes an enterprise that has yet to build a commercially viable business and is developing a concept and doing research and development.

The investors understood it would take time to move the company from the seed stage up to the next level.

See also: Angels, First-Round Financing, Front Money, Seed Capital, Seed Stage, Venture Capital, Venture Capitalists

Self-Confident
Sure of oneself and one's abilities; describes a person with a high level of self-esteem.

Although she had never spoken in front of so many people, she was self-confident enough to know she could pull off the major presentation for her team.

See also: Independent, Management Style

Self-Employed
An individual who earns income from a business that he or she owns rather than receiving a salary or wage from an employer.

The artist made less money because he was self-employed than he might have otherwise, but it allowed him to paint full time, which had always been his goal.

See also: Income, Taxes

Self-Service
A self-directed way to interact with a business; selling from a sales outlet directly to the end user, usually at prices lower than full retail price.

The business-to-consumer art Web site is a completely self-service business.

See also: Direct Marketing, End User

Seller (online)
An individual or business that sells products or services and is capable of accepting payment for products and services via an online seller's account.

Internet auction sites allow sellers to reach customers who wouldn't otherwise find the product.

See also: E-Commerce, Business to Commerce (B-to-C, B2C), Sales

Seller's Account
The bank account a seller identifies as the sole account from which monthly and/or transaction fees are debited.

The auctioneer set up a seller's account in order to receive online sales from his transactions.

See also: Bank, E-Commerce

Serious
Earnestly involved in one's endeavors; focused and directed.

She is a serious graphic artist who concentrates fully and applies herself thoroughly when developing a new product design.

See also: Focus

Served Available Market (SAM)
The portion of the total available market (TAM) that a given product or service can supply; the market that is served by a business, project, or enterprise.

In a competitive environment, it is vital that a corporation be aware of the SAM and see the market realistically.

See also: Market Share, Metrics, Total Available Market (TAM)

Server
A given host of information available on the World Wide Web that facilitates the transfer of Web pages and the user's interaction with the Web site.

Many millions of servers are connected to the Internet and run continuously throughout the world.

See also: Computer, Information, Network

Settlement

The online process of transferring funds for sales and credits between acquirers and issuers, including the final debiting of a cardholder's account, and crediting a seller's account.

With the advent of debit cards and online banking, settlements can now be arranged without ever writing a check or using the mail.

See also: Debt, Cardholder, E-Commerce, Online

Severance

Money given to employees when they are asked to leave their job; payments to executives in the event of their termination after a change in control.

The company tried to lessen the shock of closing by offering its employees generous severance packages.

See also: Golden Parachute, Layoff, Outplacement, Termination

Share of Stock

A unit of ownership in a corporation, which can be held privately or publicly.

The little boy was very proud of his share of stock in his favorite toy store even though he only had the one.

See also: Public Company, Stockholder or Shareholder

Shareholder Value

Putting shareholders first; the notion that all business activity should aim to maximize the total value of a company's shares; emphasizes profitability over responsibility and sees organizations primarily as instruments of its owners.

Some critics argue that concentrating on shareholder value will be harmful to a company's other stakeholders, such as employees, suppliers and customers.

See also: Share of Stock, Stakeholders, Stockholder or Shareholder, Value

Shoplifting

The taking of a store's merchandise by a customer who has not paid for it.

Shoplifting accounts for a large percentage of the losses incurred by retail stores.

See also: Customer, Retailer, Risk

Shopping Carts

Software that allows customers to select items from an online store and then buy them electronically.

Online shopping carts have made shopping from home easier than trekking to the mall.

See also: E-Commerce, Online

Short-Term Debt
Loans and other debt instruments that are to be repaid within one year or the current accounting period. Short-term debt is reported on the balance sheet as a current liability.

The interest charged by credit cards on short-term debt tends to be very different from the interest charged by banks on long-term debt.

See also: Balance Sheet, Current Liability, Debt, Loan, Long-Term Debt

Shutdown
Discontinuance of work due to some shortfall; breakdown, lack of parts and labor, or lack of demand for the items being produced.

The strike resulted in a three-day shutdown of the plant before the contracts were finally settled.

See also: Demand, Manufacturing, Production

Sigma
A statistical term that measures how far a given process deviates from perfection; refers to the standard deviation of a population.

Sigma is one of many measurements used in quality management to ensure that each unit is nearly identical in quality.

See also: Six Sigma, Total Quality Management (TQM)

Sign Off/Log-Off
Instructions keyed into the computer to terminate communication with the system.

Due to the confidential nature of the data, failure to log-off at the end of a shift was cause for termination.

See also: Communication, Computer, Network, Sign On/Login

Sign On/Login
Instructions keyed into the computer to open up communication with the system.

Every user was required to login on the system in order to access the database.

See also: Communication, Computer, Network, Sign Off/Log-Off

Signature Loan
A loan based on a personal guarantee requiring only a signature as collateral.

The attorney was well enough known that he was able to acquire a signature loan with ease.

See also: Debt, Debt Service, Loan, Unsecured Loan

Silent Generation

Consumers born between 1925 and 1942; characterized by a desire to minimize risk and a high need for security; these consumers tend to be withdrawn, cautious, and indifferent.

The Silent Generation is more likely to invest in long-term stocks and bonds than get involved with day trading.

See also: Cohort, Market Research, Marketing

Silent Investor

A financial partner in an organization who's unrecognized, officially or publicly, as an equity stakeholder in the venture.

Few people realized how many corporations had the philanthropist on board as a silent investor.

See also: Equity, Partner, Stakeholder

Silent Partner

A partner who has a financial interest in the company, venture, or enterprise without an active role, even though he/she may be known to the public as a partner.

The actor was a silent partner in the restaurant chain, so he made public appearances there frequently.

See also: Disclosure, Investor, Partner

Simulation and Modeling

Visualization of complex processes and the testing of concepts and designs without building physical replicas; a process that that reduces risk and uncertainty for business choices.

Instead of trying to simply explain the project, the team decided simulation and modeling would make it clearer to investors.

See also: Problem Solving, Prototype, Risk Reduction

Situation

The general state of things; the combination of circumstances at a given time; condition or position in which a group finds itself; complex, critical, or unusual difficulty.

After the dot-com bubble burst in the 1990s, the situation in the computer industry was uncertain for a few years as the industry leveled out again.

See also: Audit, Complexity, Critical, Position

Six Sigma

A methodology that provides businesses with the tools to improve the capability of their business processes. The central idea behind Six Sigma is that if you can measure how many defects you have in a process, you can systematically figure out how to eliminate them and get as close to zero defects as possible. The goal of Six Sigma is to increase profits by eliminating variability, defects, and waste that undermine customer loyalty.

As consumers have come to expect more from the technology they buy, the use of Six Sigma has become more widespread because glitches and defects are no longer an option if a company wants to stay in business.

See also: Quality, Quality Assurance, Total Quality Management (TQM)

Skill

Ability to produce solutions in some problem domain; learned competencies.

Having the skills for a job can often be more desirable than having years of education.

See also: Competencies, Learning, Solutions

Skilled

Able to carry out team or organizational tasks or techniques proficiently.

Working on the line required more than a trained monkey; it required a skilled professional who could handle the machinery.

See also: Capable, Organization, Teams

Skim the Cream

A strategy for pricing a new product or service at a high level in order to take advantage of the willingness of some consumers to pay it; a strategy for garnering quick cash (with minimal desire for significant market penetration and control) by setting your prices very high (sometimes called "skimming").

Since the movie was not expected to have long-term impact, the toy manufacturer decided to skim the cream and rushed related products to the store quickly.

See also: Market Penetration, Sales, Strategy

Small Claims Court

A court that hears and resolves minor disputes; often used by small businesses to collect debt or resolve a legal issue at a low cost.

The dressmaker took the bride to small claims court in an attempt to get the past-due payments on the wedding gown.

See also: Common Law

SMART Criteria

An acronym aimed at helping workers remember that goals and objectives should be specific, measurable, achievable, relevant, and time bound. The objective should state exactly what is to be achieved; be capable of measurement so that it is possible to determine whether (or how far) it has been achieved; be realistic given the circumstances in which it is set and available resources; be relevant to the people responsible for achieving them; and be set with a realistic time-frame in mind.

The SMART criteria were decided upon by everyone involved in the project so no one could later claim they hadn't known something.

See also: Functional Objectives, Goals, Objectives

Software

Electronic media content organizations use to operate a business through systems such as the programs and other operating information used by a computer, as well as expression of ideas such as film, tapes, records, and so on.

Software upgrades can often be downloaded for free from product-specific Web sites.

See also: Access, Computer, Decision Support Systems (DSS), System

Sole Proprietorship

An enterprise that is owned by a single individual; profit and loss are reported by the individual on his/her tax return.

The fiction writer operated her business as a sole proprietorship.

See also: Profit, Proprietorship, Structure, Tax

Solutions

Methods or actions used to resolve a user's problem; meeting a need with the correct information, system, product, or service at the right time.

The management team met once a month to address issues and find solutions to the largest difficulties within the departments.

See also: Problem Solving, Success

Spam

Unwanted, unsolicited e-mail (usually of a commercial nature sent out in bulk) with no benefit to the recipient, sent without permission, and usually irrelevant to the recipient.

She was distressed when most of her e-mail was spam instead of messages from friends.

See also: Communication, E-Mail, Internet, Portal, Search Engine, Spam Blocker

Spam Blocker

Automatic processing of incoming and outgoing emails and other messages. Also applies to the intervention by humans in addition to artificial intelligence processing and filters.

He installed a spam blocker when his daughter started receiving inappropriate e-mails in her mailbox.

See also: Artificial Intelligence, E-Mail, Internet, Spam

Speaker's Notes

Notes created in presentation software programs that are hidden to the audience and used for the reference of the presenter.

Although she was confident about her presentation, she was grateful for the speaker's notes she had with her just in case.

See also: Oral Presentations, Presentation Slides

Spider

A tool designed to help search engines to keep up with the evolution of Web content by seeking new Web sites and content.

Most search engines will spider in order to ensure the most up-to-date and accurate Web sites are presented as results.

See also: Database, Search Engine, Web Page, World Wide Web (WWW)

Sponsor

An executive decision maker in the organization who can assign resources and can make final decisions on the project, venture, or activity.

Our sponsor was the head of the nonprofit organization.

See also: Decision Making, Organizations, Project, Venture

Stable

Steady, consistent, and predictable.

After the flamboyant style of the last director, the staff was grateful for the new woman's stable, calm influence.

See also: Mature, Reliable

Stakeholders

An individual or group with an interest in the success of a group or an organization in delivering intended results and maintaining the viability of the group or organization's product and/or service. Any party that has an interest ("stake") in a firm or a legitimate interest in a project or entity.

The stakeholders were pleased with the company's progress.

See also: Organizations, Stockholder or Shareholder, Teams

Stars
Products, service positions, or situations with a high growth rate that are rising into market dominance characterized by both high market growth and share at the same time.

Even though the growth of stars will eventually slow, assuming it was not just a fad, those products have the potential to stay a major money maker for the company.

See also: Boston Consulting Group Box (BCG Box), Strategy

Start-Up
A new business or company; or the early stages of a venture, project, or product development.

The major chain was unexpectedly challenged by the lower prices offered by the start-up that opened in the neighborhood.

or

The start-up costs would have been prohibitive had the entrepreneurs not found generous investors.

See also: Angel Capital, Entrepreneurial Chaos, Seed Stage

Start-Up Stage
The beginning stage in an enterprise during which there is a need for managing planning, people, and financial resources.

During the start-up stage, Jake borrowed $10,000 from his parents, created a business plan, and hired a marketing person to get his Web business off the ground.

See also: Entrepreneur, Seed Stage, Start-Up, Venture

Statement of Work (SOW)
A description of the key elements of a project or program; a brief summary of financial aspects of a contract; technical details such as the scope, location, period of performance, deliverables, and applicable standards.

The vendor submitted a SOW to every company involved before beginning a project.

See also: Contract, Life Cycle, Project Management

Statistical Control
A methodology for achieving quality control in a manufacturing process using metrics and statistics to discover and significantly change quality.

Although the CEO appreciated the gut feelings of her experienced staff, she preferred statistical control to back up any suggestions.

See also: Quality Control, Six Sigma, Statistical, Variance

Status Quo

The existing state of affairs; absence of change.

The new department head was brought in for the purpose of shaking up the status quo.

See also: Change, Situation

Steering Committee

A group or a team that arranges or plans projects and programs for an enterprise; a leadership group to consider some issue or solve a problem.

The CEO appointed a steering committee to oversee the integration of the newly acquired company.

See also: Ad Hoc, Change Management, Problem-Solving, Task Force, Team

Stock

A unit of ownership in a company; equity in an enterprise; a claim on a share in the company's assets and profits.

Many people choose to invest their money by purchasing stock in various companies.

See also: Equity, Stockholder or Shareholder

Stock Certificate

The official document issued by the corporation to the stockholder verifying ownership in the enterprise.

Her grandfather kept all of his stock certificates in a safety deposit box at the bank.

See also: Corporation, Equity, Stock, Stockholder or Shareholder

Stock Option

A right to buy a given amount of company stock at a given price for a given period of time, on or before a certain date.

The company offered stock options as part of its employee benefits package.

See also: Deferred Compensation, Options

Stockholder or Shareholder

A person or entity that legally owns one or more shares of stock in a joint stock company. A company's shareholders collectively own that company.

Many shareholders sold their stocks when the company's unethical business practices became common knowledge.

See also: Stakeholder, Stock, Stockholder's Equity

Stockholder's Equity

The portion of a business owned by the stockholders. Reported on the balance sheet.

The family agreed to sell shares publicly so long as the stockholder's equity never rose above 40 percent.

See also: Balance Sheet, Equity, Stockholder or Shareholder

Stockout

A situation in which a company is unable to fill an order due to the item(s) being unavailable.

The unexpected demand for the video game caused a stockout during the holiday rush.

See also: Demand, Inventories, Supply

Storyboarding

A means to facilitate group communications through brainstorming and problem solving; a media for developing ideas and concepts, either with physical flip charts or using multimedia technology by collecting frames of information and sequencing them to represent a concept.

The advertising team gave a storyboarding presentation to the client in order to show them the design of the commercial.

See also: Brainstorming, Communications, Flowchart, Multimedia, Teams

Straight-Line Depreciation

A method of depreciation in which capital cost is amortized in equal periodic amounts over the estimated life of an asset.

Measured with straight-line depreciation, the printer would be worthless in three years even though its warranty covered it for five.

See also: Capital Gains, Depreciation, Income Statement

Strategic Analysis

Analyzing the basic position and external and internal factors that drive a business; goals are analyzed to determine the factors that affect their achievement.

The strategic analysis indicated the firm could earn several million dollars within the next few years.

See also: Analysis, Critical Success Factors (CSFs), Strategic Choices, Strategic Management, Strategic Objectives, Strategic Success Factors (SSFs), Strategy

Strategic Business Unit (SBU)

A unit of the company that has a separate mission and objectives and that can be planned independently from the other businesses. An SBU can be a company division, a product line, or even individual brands—it all depends on how the company is organized.

Few people realized that the small firm that specialized in poverty law was simply an SBU of the larger corporate firm.

See also: Boston Consulting Group Box (BCG Box), Organizations, Strategy

Strategic Choices

Leadership decisions in which the option selected would be difficult to impossible to reverse once implementation is underway. Significant organizational resources are committed, and the decisions often result in leadership role changes.

The executives took their time with the strategic choices because they knew their decisions would affect the company for the next decade.

See also: Scenario, Strategic Management, Strategy, Strategy Implementation, Synergy, Trade-Off

Strategic Inflection Points

Points in time when strategic change, internal or external, change the paradigm for an organization; major obstacles or opportunities for making a strategic choice; that which causes a fundamental change in business strategy.

While it is usually easy to pinpoint strategic inflection points using hindsight, a smart investor or business person can recognize them at the time they occur.

See also: 10X Change, Strategic Choices

Strategic Intent

The means by which an organization will achieve its vision; future-oriented and outside the range of planning.

The CEO kept her eye on the strategic intent of her firm and didn't let petty distractions take her energy.

See also: Goals, Planning, Strategy, Vision

Strategic Management

Making strategic choices or decisions; the management of marketplace strategy, the organization, and the connections between them.

Each of the departments had strategies for meeting the deadlines so the director had to handle the strategic management of ensuring they all came together.

See also: Business Intelligence, Business Philosophy, Organizations, Strategic Analysis, Strategic Choice, Strategy, Strategy Implementation

Strategic Objectives

Major goals that affect the entity's overall direction and viability.

Before the company could work out of its slump and become successful again, the board of directors had to agree on new strategic objectives.

See also: Critical Success Factors (CSFs), Rivalry Among Industry Competitors, Strategic Management

Strategic Options/Alternatives

The available choices a leader has to implement a strategy, vision, or goal.

Although the manager was adept at following a set plan, he was not as skilled at recognizing new strategic options if the original plan failed.

See also: Strategic Choices, Strategic Management, Strategic Planning, Strategy

Strategic Planning

A management process for setting the strategic direction of an enterprise or organization; developing strategies to reach a defined objective; guiding an organization intelligently into the future. The objective of strategic planning is to set the direction of a business and create its shape so that the products and services it provides meet the overall business objectives.

The corporation decided to create and hire a new position to oversee the managers to assist with the day-to-day operations of the company and enable the founders and senior managers to focus more on strategic planning and execution.

See also: Competitive Advantage, Strategic Options/Alternatives, Strategy

Strategic Scope

The boundaries of operations; "what" and "how" the enterprise, company, firm, business unit, venture, or program exists; how the constituent's or stakeholder's interests are balanced; and the incorporation of management's vision and nature of the business.

The board scaled back the strategic scope of the company when it became obvious the expansion had been poorly planned.

See also: Mission, Purpose, Values, Vision

Strategic Success Factors (SSFs)

The characteristics, conditions, or variables that can have a significant impact on the success of a firm competing in a particular industry.

In looking at all the SSFs, the business decided to begin its overseas expansion in Asia rather than Europe.

See also: Market Factors, Strategic Analysis, Strategic Choices, Strategic Management, Strategic Options/Alternatives, Strategy

Strategy

The long-term direction and scope of an organization; the plan to achieve advantage in the industry and meet the expectation of stakeholders; addresses the connection between the organization and the marketplace.

The ad campaign strategy was very different in the United States than abroad because of the FCC guidelines.

See also: Competitive Advantage, Long-Term Goals, Organization, Purpose, Scope, Stakeholders, Strategic Management

> **Strategy** has to be based on information about markets, customers, and non-customers; about technology in one's own industry and others; about worldwide finance; and about the changing world economy.

Strategy Implementation

Making strategy work; actions taken to carry out a plan for achieving goals; linking a vision to operational plans and budgets.

They made a good team because he was a visionary and she was excellent at strategy implementation.

See also: Resource Allocation, Strategic Analysis, Strategic Choices, Strategic Management, Strategic Objectives, Strategy

Streaming

A means to allow users to play audio and video files that have been downloaded from the Internet or a network.

The radio station knew that streaming audio content on its Web site would be a good way to attract listeners from all over the country, not just the local area.

See also: Browser, Internet, Multimedia

Streamline

Methods to save money and grind out ideas that boost revenue.

The plant needed to be streamlined in order for production to be as efficient as required to meet the new order.

See also: Efficiency, Productivity

Structure

The way in which the organization's units and teams relate to each other. Structures may be centralized, functional divisions (top-down structure), decentralized, or may take the form of a matrix, network, holding, and so on.

The board of directors took the retirement and resignation of several of the management team as an opportunity to change the entire structure of the company.

See also: Decentralized, Functional, Matrix, Organizations, Teams, Top-Down

Subcontract

An arrangement allowing a third party to come in and complete all or part of the work indicated in the original contract.

The construction firm chose to subcontract out the plumbing aspect of a job rather than keep plumbers on staff.

See also: Contract, Supplier, Vendor

Substitute

A product or service that replaces an existing competitor; two kinds of goods that can be consumed or used in place of one another, in at least some of their possible uses.

A PDA is a useful substitute for a laptop when staff members are away from the site temporarily.

See Also: Consumers, Demand, Economics, Suppliers

Success

The achievement of something desired, planned, or attempted; an accomplishment.

The first time the woman sat behind her own desk in her own office, she felt like a success.

See also: Accomplishment, Goal, Leadership

Success can be many things. Each of us can experience **success.** It begins with a vision, a dream that provides a goal and a direction—a perspective to view our behavior. **Success** is a journey rather than a destination. **Success** is living your dreams. The art of **success** is available to everyone. Each individual has his own perception of **success.** Groups and organizations have a mission that defines **success** for them.

Succession

The gradual and orderly process of change in an organization brought about by the progressive replacement of one leader by another until a stable climax is established.

The firm grew to national prominence in part because of a succession of intelligent and savvy CEOs.

See also: Authority, Business Planning, Conflict Resolution, Leadership Selection, Legacy, Responsibility

Suggesting Box/Suggestion Box

A designated place in a company where employees can anonymously place suggestions regarding company policies, procedures, and activities.

The suggestion box hung just outside the restrooms so it wouldn't be obvious if a staff member dropped a note in.

See also: Employee, Motivation, Team Building

Supplier

Businesses that supply materials and other products to an industry.

The supplier list included several raw materials vendors.

See also: Supply, Supply Chain, Vendor

Supplier Bargaining Power

The influence suppliers have over the competitors in a given industry.

Supplier bargaining power increases when demand increases, and it decreases when demand decreases.

See also: Competitive Advantage, Porter's Five-Force Model, Strategy

Supply

The total amount of a good or service available for purchase by consumers.

Some companies will limit the supply of luxury goods in order to make owning the item even more of a status symbol.

See also: Demand, Economics

Supply Chain

A method of collaborating horizontally with the chain of suppliers, manufacturers, wholesalers, distributors, and stores that enable a product to be made, sold, and delivered; includes business strategy, information flow, and system compatibility.

If any part of the plant's supply chain broke down, the production would come to a complete stop until the issue was resolved.

See also: Alliance, Collaboration, Supplier, Supply, Supply Chain Management

Supply Chain Management

Planning, organizing, and controlling all the steps in the manufacturing and/or distribution process.

Each vendor had a single person handling supply chain management so no step was missed and communication never broke down.

See also: Relationship, Supply Chain

Supportive

Helpful; advocating, encouraging in the work place.

The entire staff was very supportive of the new manager as she got settled into her new position.

See also: Cooperative, Helpful

Suppress

To place under management control; keep under control; keep in check; keep from public knowledge by various means.

The CEO did everything in his power to suppress the rumor that the company was being taken over.

See also: Control, Pent-Up Demand

Sustainability

The integration of economic progress, social development, and environmental concerns with the objective of ensuring a quality of life for future generations at least as good as today's.

Recently, there has been much concern about the sustainability of fossil fuels and the impact their use will have on the environment.

See also: Economics, Microeconomics

SWOT Analysis

A tool that identifies the strengths, weaknesses, opportunities, and threats of an organization; an assessment of a business's internal position and external environmental influences. Method of developing a plan that takes into consideration many different internal and external factors; maximizes the potential of the strengths and opportunities while minimizing the impact of the weaknesses and threats.

The scheduled activity during the afternoon of the retreat was for each group to perform a SWOT analysis and bring them to the whole group.

See also: Opportunities, Strategic Management, Strategy, Threat

Symbol

An arbitrary sign (written or printed) that has acquired a conventional significance; something visible to stakeholders that by association or convention represents something else that is invisible.

The young woman saw getting her own office as a symbol of how far she had come in the company.

See also: Brand, Logo, Trademarks

Syndication

The supplying of information or content for simultaneous publication in several periodicals or Web sites.

Getting picked up for syndication is the goal of every comic-strip writer.

See also: Investor, Risk

Synergy

Creating value through alliances, working on the theory that two companies combined will be greater than the sum of the separate individual parts. Creative cooperation, or the principle that collaborating toward attaining a purpose often achieves more than could be achieved by organizations working independently.

The synergy that developed after the merger was greater than even the participants had expected.

See also: Collaboration, Mergers and Acquisitions (M&A), Value Creation

System

An organized structure for arranging or classifying; an assemblage of elements comprising a whole with each element related to other elements. Organizations are viewed as human systems of interacting components such as subsystems, processes, and organizational structures.

Records of the values of each account in the balance sheet are maintained using a system of accounting known as double-entry bookkeeping.

See also: Organizations, Processes, Structure

Systematic

Orderly; characterized by order and planning.

The team, left alone for so long, was not used to the new director's systematic way of addressing every issue.

See also: Organized, Planning

Systems Thinking
An approach for studying and managing complex feedback systems, such as that found in business and other social systems.

The board hired an expert in systems thinking in an attempt to make the disparate departments a more united, functioning whole.

See also: Feedback, Learning Organization

> By seeing the whole picture, teams are better able to think of new possibilities that they may not have come up with previously, in spite of their best efforts. **Systems thinking** has the power to help teams create insights like this, when applied well to a suitable problem. When making strategic decisions, narrow choices to the most important factors that drive value creation.

T

Tactful
Discreet; able to handle people and situations delicately and considerately so that no one is offended, hurt, or embarrassed.

The attorney knew she had to be tactful when dealing with the other side's negotiating team.

See also: Leadership. Professional

Take-One
A coupon or mail-order offer attached to a product as incentive for future purchase at a discount or bonus.

One of the most successful ad campaigns in the company's history was the take-one offer included in every six-pack.

See also: Advertising, Marketing

Takeover
The result of a purchase of one company by another; referring to transfer of control of a firm from one group of shareholder's to another group of shareholders.

Although the two companies actually merged, it was seen by the general public as a takeover because of the larger firm's reputation.

See also: Acquisition, Arbitrage, Buyout, Merger

Target Market

The market selected for penetration by a firm's management; a specified audience or demographic group that an ad, product, or service is intended to reach.

The game's target market was originally teenagers, but it soon became popular with adults as well.

See also: Marketing, Market, Served Market

Task

A portion of a project; a specific effort leading toward an objective; a means in which management assigns work and activities.

Although dull, the menial tasks can be as important to a project's success as the larger, more interesting ones.

See also: Project Management, Schedule, Milestone

Task Force

A temporary group, team, or organization formed to accomplish a particular objective; groups of employees that meet regularly to come up with solutions to problems concerning processes and productivity.

A task force was created to address the recordkeeping issues staff had complained about by streamlining the forms and condensing the databases.

See also: Quality Circles, Teams

Taxes (Tax)

The a financial charge or other levy imposed on an individual or a legal entity, levied by the government on workers' income and business profits or added to the cost of some goods, services, and transactions.

Almost everyone who does business or earns an income in the United States is required to pay taxes to the federal government.

See also: EBIDA, Economics, Taxable Income

Tax Benefits

The deductions, protection, savings, and shelters that result from investing in a business.

The tax benefits weren't great enough for the woman to be willing to invest in the small company.

See also: Investing, Taxes

Tax Credit

A dollar-for-dollar reduction in tax. Can be deducted directly from taxes owed.
The state offered a tax credit to any business willing to open a plant or office in the struggling community.
See also: Credit, Taxes

Tax Deduction

A part of a person's or business's expenses that reduces income subject to tax.
As an artist, he could list his supplies and studio fees as tax deductions.
See also: Expenses, Taxes

Tax Preference Item

An item that must be included when calculating the alternative minimum tax.
The IRS created tax preference items to ensure businesses pay something, even if it is just the alternative minimum tax.
See also: Income Tax, Taxes

Taxable Income

The amount of income or profit left after all allowable business deductions and exemptions have been subtracted. This remaining income is taxable.
Since the man had so many deductions, his taxable income was lower than he had originally expected.
See also: Deduction, Exemptions, Income Tax, Taxes

Team Building

Organizing a collection of individuals with the goal of having them perform better as a group; putting people together for a job; establishing and developing a greater sense of collaboration and trust between team members.
The department paid for the program staff to go on team building outings.
See also: Culture, Group Processes, Organizations, Team Player, Teams, Teamwork

Team Player

A person who is skilled at assuming multiple roles, stepping up to do whatever it takes to get the job done on time and on budget—without breaking the rules. One who complements the other members of a team and helps them perform better. As a result of the team player's efforts, the entire team executes and exceeds expectations.
Although his personality could be abrasive, no one could say he was anything but a team player.
See also: A-Team, Behavior, Teams, Teamwork

Teams

A group organized to work together linked in a common purpose. A term adapted from sports and applied to organizations. Teams are especially appropriate for conducting tasks that are high in complexity and have many interdependent subtasks.

The project staff was broken up into smaller teams so that more could get done in less time.

See also: Team Building, Team Player, Teamwork

Teamwork

A cooperative effort by members of a group or team to achieve a common goal; cooperative work done by a team.

Employees need training to make the transition from individually focused work to teamwork.

See also: Management Team, Team Building, Team Player, Teams

Technical Obsolescence

A product or service that is no longer in demand because of a new, superior technology or innovation.

Touch-tone dialing sent rotary phones into technical obsolescence the same way rotary phones once replaced operated-assisted phone lines.

See also: Market, Near-Term Market, Obsolescence, Opportunities, Product Obsolescence, Technology

Technological Uncertainty

Any risks or unknowns inherent in the technology being used for a project. Levels of technological uncertainty and the time needed to correct it must be accounted for at all stages of the project.

NASA calculates technological uncertainty into every launch it makes of exploratory vehicles but still carries the hope that every program and piece of equipment works in space the way it worked on Earth.

See also: Project, Risk, Uncertainty

Technology

The process of developing practical applications for the results of scientific research and applied engineering; the material entities created by the application of disciplines dealing with the art or science of applying scientific knowledge to practical problems.

Due to the speed of advancement, that which is cutting-edge technology today may very well be obsolete in only five years.

See also: Innovation, Technology Transfer

T

Technology Insertion

Using technologically advanced subsystems to increase the value of the product to the user.

The computer technician recommended a technology insertion that would replace the basic hard drive with a DVD read/write drive.

See also: End User, Obsolescence, Technology

Technology Transfer

The practice of taking laboratory developments and creating marketable products from those innovations; or adapting products based on a certain technology for use in a different field.

It took years for the technology transfer between the enormous computers originally designed to become small enough to be reasonable for private consumers.

or

As patients began to report that antidepressants cut back on the cravings for cigarettes, a technology transfer seemed inevitable.

See also: Innovation, Marketing, Technology

Teleconferencing

A medium for communications between two or more remote locations using audio via telephone or Internet; a meeting conducted by telephone among people in different locations.

Since the partners were in three separate parts of the country, they used teleconferencing instead of trying to meet every time an issue arose.

See also: Communication, Internet, Meeting

Telemarketing

A direct marketing technique using a combination of computers and telephones to sell products/services in which a consumer is called by a seller, or the consumer calls the seller, the product or service is described, and the consumer decides whether or not to purchase.

Call centers are used by telemarketing companies and any large enterprise that uses the telephone to sell or service products and services.

See also: Direct Marketing

Temporary Employee

A person employed for a limited time period who is often paid by a third party; someone who fills a shortage or need in a firm's staff.

The firm brought in a temporary employee to cover the receptionist's position while she was on maternity leave.

See also: Employee, Labor Pool

Term Loan

A loan with an original maturity beyond one year. Reported on the balance sheet as a long-term liability.

The entrepreneurs qualified for a term loan based on the strength of their proposal and previously established credit rating.

See also: Balance Sheet, Loan, Long-Term Liabilities

Term Sheet

A summary of the principal conditions for a proposed investment by a venture capital firm in a company; the essence of an acquisition transaction; a communication between an investor and an entrepreneur.

The first step in the merger was for the two companies to write up a term sheet.

See also: Acquisition, Entrepreneur, Investment, Venture Capital

Termination

Cancellation of an agreement or contract or employment; the point in time at which something ends.

She was able to return the laptop because the warranty termination hadn't occurred yet.

See also: At-Will Employment, Cancellation, Employee, Exit Interview, Layoff, Outplacement

Terminology

A system of words used in business, management, and leadership.

If you are not in a field, the specific terminology used in that industry can be intimidating and confusing.

See also: Business Literacy, Nomenclature, Terms

Terms

The parameters of a deal; the time limits and amount to be paid; conditions for paying an invoice.

According to the terms of the contract, the owners of the company would receive both cash and stocks in the new business once the sale was complete.

See also: Agreement, Bill of Sale, Contract, Invoices, Period, Term Sheet

Testimonial

An endorsement of a product or service by someone who has credibility in the market sector or industry, such as a satisfied customer or a celebrity.

The store posted testimonials from previous customers on its Web site so prospective customers could read the reviews.

See also: Customer, Endorsement, Success

Think Digital, Act Analog

The theory that a business should use all the digital tools at its disposal—computers, Web sites, instruments—to create great products while making the products useful and easy to use by the end user.

Developers thought digital and acted analog when creating the most popular and user-friendly music- and movie-download Web sites.

See also: Bootstrapping, Digital Manufacturing, Entrepreneur, Innovation

Threats

Negative risks that may or may not occur; opposed to opportunities, which are positive risks.

After identifying and addressing the threats involved, the board decided the project was worth launching.

See also: Opportunities, Risk, Situation, Strategy, SWOT Analysis

Time Horizon

A point in the future at which some plan or activity is assumed to end.

Whenever two or more groups work together for the first time, it is important to set a time horizon in order to ensure everyone is on the same timeline.

See also: Milestone, Period, Risk Management, Scenario

Time Management

A philosophy and a methodology for optimization of daily work schedules for maximum productivity and efficiency.

Employees in their first jobs must learn time management skills quickly or else get overwhelmed by the difference in school requirements and business ones.

See also: Activity Sequencing, Goal, Objectives, Obstacles, Organization, Resource Allocation, Scheduling, Task

Time-to-Market

The period of time between a product or service concept and when it's put into use by the end user.

After the success of the prototype, the team hoped to shorten the time-to-market estimate.

See also: Innovation, Lead Time, Product Development, Product Life Cycle Management, Project Management, Risk

Time Value of Money

The concept that, provided money can earn interest, any amount of money is worth more the sooner it is received. The support for this concept is that money commands interest, either imputed or explicit. Interest costs are a function of the interest rate and the time for which the money is being rented (used). Time value of money (TVM) is an important concept in financial management. It can be used to compare investment alternatives and to solve problems involving loans, mortgages, leases, savings, and annuities.

Although she came to regret paying her advisor at the beginning of the project, she knew the time value of money only made it fair that she do so.

See also: Discounted Cash Flow, Extrinsic Value, Future Value, Interest, Intrinsic Value, Net Present Value (NPV)

> Time literally is money—the value of the money you have now is not the same as it will be worth in the future, and vice versa. It is therefore important to know how to calculate the **time value of money** so that you can distinguish between the worth of investments that offer you returns at different times.

Timesheet

A method for recording the amount of a team member's time spent on each activity.

Every employee was expected to turn in a completed timesheet each Friday.

See also: Employee, Invoice, Payroll

Tipping Point

A point of no return; a threshold at which the status quo has changed; the beginning of a major shift or discontinuity; often, the point in which markets are redefined.

The producer truly believed the band was at the tipping point of their career, so he wanted to sign with them before another label got them first.

See also: Strategic Inflection Points, Strategy, Strategic Change

Top Management

Executives who plan, organize, control, and lead an organization.

The top management worked very hard at not losing touch with what lower-level staff dealt with on a daily basis.

See also: Chief Executive Officer (CEO)

Top-Down

An approach to planning that involves a high degree of top-management involvement; an estimating technique that uses historical project information to estimate the project duration of a similar project.

The director believed in a top-down style of management and so always knew exactly what was going on in every department.

See also: Budget, Business Plan, Organizations, Planning, Structure

Total Available Market (TAM)

The total of the potential customers within a market who have the capacity to buy a product or service.

Although the TAM for high-end, luxury items is relatively small, demand among those customers is high enough to ensure continued production.

See also: Market Share, Metrics, Served Available Market (SAM)

Total Quality Management (TQM)

A management strategy aimed at embedding awareness of quality in all organizational processes; an integrated approach to organizational improvement and to increasing production and service quality, whose core ideas include doing things right the first time, striving for continuous improvement, and a devotion to understanding and meeting customer needs.

Although the attitudes behind TQM seem simplistic and almost habitual, at the time it was introduced it was considered groundbreaking.

See also: Goals, Organizations, Production, Productivity, Quality, Quality Circles, Resource Allocation

Track Record

What has happened before; athletic metaphor for an individual's history of performance in any given field.

The consultant's track record for turning flagging companies into thriving ones was excellent and kept her in demand.

See also: Accomplishment, Performance, Mature

Trade Association

A not-for-profit organization that exists to support its members.

Usually, people who belong to a trade association work in closely related occupations.

See also: Benchmark, Nonprofit Corporation (Not-for-profit), Organizations, Relationships

Trade Discount

A discount on the list price of merchandise before the credit terms apply, allowed only to specific customers.

Trade discounts are used to encourage prompt payment.

See also: Credit, Payments

Trade Secret

Any type of information, including a formula, pattern, compilation, program, device, method, technique, or process, that derives independent value from not being generally known to other persons who could obtain economic value from its disclosure or use.

Many corporations require employees to sign agreements stating they will not sell trade secrets, even in cases of termination of employment.

See also: Disclosure, Intellectual Property

Trade Show

A segment- or industry-wide marketplace where many manufacturers and suppliers demonstrate and market their products and services, actively solicit sales, and build relationships.

Plans were made for the new technology to be released to the public at three different trade shows nationwide.

See also: Marketplace, Relationships, Trade Associations

Trade-Off

A method of selecting between two or more alternatives; losing one quality or aspect of something in return for gaining another quality or aspect; relating to opportunity cost, involves a sacrifice that must be made to obtain something.

The promotion was a fair trade-off for having to relocate cross-country.

See also: Decision Making, Opportunity Cost, Strategic Choices, Strategy

Trademarks

The name, brand, or part of a brand of a product or service that has been legally registered as the property of an enterprise. A name, phrase, logo, image, or combination of images used to identify and distinguish a business from others in the marketplace.

Developing a unique and instantly recognizable trademark is a proven marketing technique.

See also: Brand, Marketing

Trailblazer

Someone who helps to open up a new market, line of research, technology, or art.

Her contributions to the field made her a trailblazer in the industry.

See also: Cutting Edge, Innovating

Trainee

Any person who is being groomed for a new role; an enrollee in a training program who is being prepared for a specific job.

The corporation was careful about choosing trainees to bring into the management program.

See also: Coaching, Leadership Development, Learning Curve, Peter Principle

Transfer Pricing

Pricing between divisions or businesses within a corporation; what one unit charges the other for products and services in order to determine each unit's profit or loss.

Businesses spend a fortune on advisers to help them set their transfer prices so that they minimize their total tax bill.

See also: Corporation, Division, Price, Strategic Business Unit (SBU), Taxes

Treasury Stock

The stock of a company held in its treasury for general corporate purposes, such as funding acquisitions or repaying debt.

The acquisition of the new division required a combination of treasury stock and cash.

See also: Corporation, Mergers and Acquisitions (M&A), Stock

True North

A direction set by leadership; an ultimate goal; an unyielding place.

One of the first things the new CEO needed to do was set a true north for the company that every employee could recognize and keep in mind when developing ventures.

See also: Direction, Focus, Goals, Leadership

Trustee

Someone who has charge of an asset for another person or organization; a legal entity that holds money or property for the benefit of someone else.

The will specified that the attorney would be the trustee of the children's accounts until they turned twenty-one.

See also: Assets, Property

Trustworthiness
Deserving of confidence.

A person can prove his trustworthiness by fulfilling an assigned responsibility.

See also: Integrity, Leadership, Reliable, Responsibility, Values

Turf
An organization's or individual's protected space or territory, such as a market, intellectual property, methods, or brand. Something that differentiates from a rival.

The company chose to formalize its association with the online site as a way of protecting its turf by publicly announcing what had been an informal partnership.

See also: Brand, Brand Equity, Brand Loyalty

Turnaround
A reversal of a negative trend; what a business organization experiences when its management team moves it from a troubled state to a positive situation.

The turnaround in consumer spending was one of the first indications the recession was coming to an end.

See also: Change Management, Organizations, Teams

Turnkey Operation
A product or project that is complete and ready for use. All the end user has to do is "turn a key" to get started.

He was willing to become a partner in the restaurant only because it was a turnkey operation and would require no fundraising legwork on his part.

See also: End User, Product, Project

Turnover
The rate that an organization changes; a ratio of the number of employees that have to be replaced in a given time period to the average number of employees; the rate at which inventory is moved or changed.

The high turnover at the nonprofit was not caused by the low paychecks but by the unreasonable demands of the director.

See also: Change, Employee, Inventories

U

Uncertainty

Being unsettled or in doubt; being unsure of an outcome, forecast, or plan; involving a situation that has unknown probabilities.

The uncertainty following the scandal made investors wary about buying industry stocks, even at the low prices.

See also: Forecast, Outcome, Risk

Underemployed

A situation in which a person is working at a job for which he or she is overqualified.

The number of underemployed workers tends to increase during a recession.

See also: Employ, Employee, Labor Pool

Understanding

A grasp of a situation; the capacity for rational thought, inference, or discrimination; comprehension, discernment, and empathy; or a statement, whether oral or written, of an exchange of promises or agreements.

Her friend spent several hours on the phone with her until she was confident in her understanding of the concepts she needed to know to complete the job.

or

They had an understanding that he would assist her with the wording of the documents and she would acknowledge him in the work.

See also: Agreements, Discrimination, Inference, Situation

Unemployment Rate

The proportion of the workforce that has lost employment in the last month or that has unsuccessfully sought a job during that time; expressed as percentage.

A rising unemployment rate is an indicator for analysts that a country may be heading into a recession.

See also: Leading Indicators, Workforce

Uniform Resource Locator (URL)

Address of a Web site; string that supplies the Internet address of a Web site or resource; a string of characters (always beginning with http://) that identifies the location of every page, graphic image, and file on the World Wide Web.

A user must know the URL for a site before it can be typed into a browser.

See also: Browser, Web Page, World Wide Web (WWW)

Union

A labor organization whose major objective is to promote members' interests when negotiating with employers.

Although they are currently somewhat controversial, it is undeniable that unions originally brought workers many key benefits and rights.

See also: Collective Bargaining, Negotiation, Organization

Uniqueness

The characteristic of being unlike anything else. Often the reason a user or consumer chooses one product/service over another.

In a field of similar products, finding and marketing a product's uniqueness can be the difference between mediocre sales and strong ones.

See also: Consumer, End User, Marketing

Unit Cost

The cost incurred in the production of one unit of product; usually computed by dividing total production cost by the number of units produced for a given time period.

An entire project may be scrapped if the unit cost of each item is too high to turn a decent profit.

See also: Manufacturing, Production, Productivity

Unpredictability

Absence of a calculable outcome; uncertainty.

Financial crises in other countries can cause a certain amount of unpredictability in the U.S. economy.

See also: Chaos, Entrepreneurial Chaos, Outcome, Uncertainty

Unsecured Loan

A loan granted solely on the strength of the maker's signature; also called a signature loan.

Since unsecured loans are generally risky, few lenders are willing to offer them to unknown businesses.

See also: Credit, Debt, Loan

Upload

Transfer of information from one computer or system to another; moving a file from a client to a server.

One of the challenges faced by software designers is ensuring accurate uploads are available for many different systems.

See also: Computer, Network

Usability

Making things user friendly; how easily a thing can be used; measure of a user's ability to complete tasks with effectiveness, efficiency, and satisfaction.

Although technicians in the computer industry loved the new software, its general usability was low so it never caught on with the general public.

See also: Effectiveness, Efficiency, Task, End User

User Friendly

The quality of being easy to understand or use; describes something customers like and enjoy using.

Any new technology must ensure it is advanced enough to meet the needs of a more savvy population but still user friendly enough to be accessible to everyone.

See also: End User, Understanding

User Groups

An informal organization formed to share information about a common technology, system, software or other business tool; group members collaborate to improve their productivity and share common experiences.

When the company switched to a computer program he didn't know, he checked with the members of his user group to find out if any of them had experience with the new program.

See also: Collaboration, Group Discussion, Informal Organization, Portal

User Interface

The means of being productive with a computer, network, or system; the way people communicate with machines.

New technologies are offering smaller and smaller user interfaces, making staying connected easier than ever.

See also: Computers, Interface, Productivity, User

V

Vacation

A period of time when an employee separates him or herself from work and pursues personal interests. The amount of vacation time an employee receives is usually defined in the contract or company policy as well as the amount of pay received for this period.

Most businesses increase the amount of vacation employees receive the longer they are with the company.

See also: Compensation, Employee

Vacation Pay

Compensation received by an employee for approved time taken off from work.

Vacation pay is often one of the benefits applicants consider before accepting a position.

See also: Compensation, Compensation Plan or Package, Rewards Employee, Vacation

Valuation

The act or process of determining the value of a business, business ownership interest, security, or intangible asset; value given to a private or public company. It is obtained most basically by multiplying the price per share (or most recent amount paid for shares) by the total number of shares outstanding.

Business valuations are also important when seeking investment capital, taking on a partner, or selling shares.

See also: Book Value, Mergers and Acquisitions (M&A), Risk

Value Added

The process of enhancing a basic product; a way of assigning value at each stage of production.

The online bookstore provides value added to its customers because it offers a larger selection of titles than any physical store could carry.

See also: Production, Product, Value

Value-Based Management

Management that is dependent on corporate purpose and values; the alignment of key organizational processes such as strategic planning, budgeting, compensation, performance measurement, training, and communication around value creation.

The entrepreneurs decided to run the business with value-based management from the very beginning in order to impress upon the whole staff how important environmental responsibility was to them and the company.

See also: Budgeting, Communication, Management, Mission, Purpose, Strategic Planning, Value Creation, Values

Value Chain

Those activities that, when combined, define a business process that a company performs to design, produce, market, deliver, and support its product.

The value chain the new management team put in place for all the new products made the company more successful than ever.

See also: Critical Success Factors (CSFs), Strategy, Supply Chain

Value Creation

Increase of the capacity to grow an enterprise. Results from effective strategic choices; comes from the design and development of new customers, the understanding of the customers' needs and requirements, and a commitment to fulfill those needs in an effective manner.

Value creation, not just profit, was very important to the owners of the winery.

See also: Clients, Competitive Advantage, Customer, Product Development, Strategy

Value Proposition

A clear statement of the tangible results a customer gets from using a product or service; a statement created to influence the customer's buying decision summarizing the customer segment, competitor targets, and the core differentiation of one's product from the offerings of competitors.

The shipping company included cost, reliability, and confidentiality in its value proposition to prospective customers.

See also: Business Plan, Competitive Advantage, Marketing, Strategy

Values

The basic beliefs of the people in the organization. Statement of why the enterprise, company, firm, business unit, venture, or program was created, representing a broad range of goals from ethics to customer service to product quality; how the constituent's or stakeholder's interests are balanced; and the incorporation of management's roles and mission.

Many socially conscious job seekers will only apply to companies whose values are in line with their own.

See also: Mission, Purpose, Strategic Scope, Vision

Variable Cost

A cost that changes in total in direct proportion to productive output or any other volume measure.

The oil business is risky because of the variable cost inherent in keeping production stable.

See also: Marginal Cost, Production

Variance

The difference between actual and planned values.

The production line had a positive variance when the team increased its productivity from the previous quarter.

See also: Actual, Planning, Program Evaluation and Review Techniques (PERT)

Variance Analysis
A management process or tool for comparing planned operational or project results against actual results, determining the impact of the variance and implementing corrective actions if needed.

The team performed a detailed variance analysis to determine why the gross margins on their product had slipped from the previous month.

See also: Actual, Business Plan, Project

Vendor
The supply source of raw materials or finished goods throughout the production and distribution processes.

The wedding planner worked with several different vendors to ensure the flowers, food, and decorations were exactly as the couple had envisioned.

See also: Production, Raw Materials, Supplier

Venture
A business, enterprise, or endeavor that involves a high level of risk and chance.

Although the man was nervous about quitting his job to start the new venture, he was also excited and ready for the challenge.

See also: Reward, Risk, Venture Capital

Venture Capital
Financing for new businesses; private equity to help new companies grow; equity money from investment pools or firms that specialize in financing the growth of young companies, usually in return for stock.

The project was promising enough that the entrepreneurs had no problem raising the venture capital they needed.

See also: Entrepreneur, Equity, Innovation, Risk, Venture

Venture Capitalist
An investor who provides early financing to new ventures with an innovative product, unique value proposition, and the prospect of rapid and profitable growth.

The venture capitalist was always on the lookout to get in on the ground floor of an exciting new business.

See also: Equity Financing, Seed Capital, Venture Capital

Vertical Integration

The extent to which an organization controls its inputs and the distribution of its products and services. Such an organization controls many or all major functions of a business, from raw materials to distribution of finished products.

Some activists accuse certain clothing retailers of vertical integration because the company controls not only the assembly sites but also the manufacturing sites and the farms where the cotton is grown.

See also: Distribution, Strategy, Value Chain

Vertical Market

A market that meets the needs of a particular industry; typically competitive due to the overlapping focuses of the products and services that are provided to the public by the participants.

A company that can become valuable to two or three vertical markets will almost inevitably find success.

See also: Competitive Position, Market

Vested

Having the rights of ownership of an asset even though the possession of those rights may be delayed until a future date.

Most companies require an employee to be employed for a specific amount of time before becoming fully vested in the retirement plans.

See also: Annuity, Pension Plan

Video Conferencing

A business meeting using technology to visually connect two or more people, groups, or organizations that are located at a distance from each other.

The team members were able to share their ideas through video conferencing since they were scattered throughout the country.

See also: Conference, Meeting, Network

Virtual Private Network (VPN)

The means by which businesses connect geographically dispersed organizations and people; a private enterprise communications network that is configured within a public network in order to take advantage of the economies of scale and management facilities of large networks.

It was easy for her office to hook their VPN into her home network so she could telecommute two days a week.

See also: Authentication, Client, Firewall, Internet, Local Area Network (LAN), Network, Security, Server, Wide Area Network (WAN)

Vision

The foresight to describe a set of ends and expected outcomes so that an organization and its leaders can formulate means and options for their implementation.

Although the nonprofit worked very locally, its vision was a global one.

See also: Leadership, Management, Organization

Visionaries

Leaders who are able to communicate and integrate their thoughts and ideas with others to form new win-win relationships that elevate individuals, teams, and organizations to new levels of achievement; people who are able to understand the meaning of trends in markets, economies, technologies, and competitive pressures.

Many businesspeople who were originally considered impractical are eventually acknowledged as visionaries.

See also: Market Factors, Organizations, Strategy, Teams, Vision

Visual Aid

A presentation tool, usually graphic in nature (such as slides or an image, graph, chart, or animation), that supports the delivery of information; a way to get a point across more effectively.

Although a visual aid may enhance a presentation, it cannot be effective if the speaker is incompetent or simply boring.

See also: Flipchart, Oral Presentations, Presentation Graphics, Presentation Slides

Visualizing

The process of creating a mental picture or vision of a future state or outcome.

The artist always spent several hours visualizing his next piece before he began work on it.

See also: Outcome, Vision, Visionaries

Voice Over IP (VOIP)

The Internet protocol that allows for telephone conversations over the Internet; digital voice communications through the World Wide Web (WWW).

The couple found VOIP an inexpensive way to stay in touch while he was traveling.

See also: Internet, Internet Protocol (IP), Network

Voicemail

An automated service that answers phone calls and records incoming messages. Enhanced voicemail services add features such as personalized greetings, longer recording times, and more saved messages.

He always had several messages on his voicemail when he arrived back in the office after lunch.

See also: Communication

Volatility

The rate of change of the stock market to market factors.

The current volatility of the stock market made the woman decide to wait until it stabilized before investing.

See also: Investment, Market Factors

Vortal

A site on the Internet that leads to other sites with information and resources about one topic or sector, as opposed to horizontal portals opening onto a wide range of topics; a way of catering to consumers' focused-environment preferences.

Vortals are especially helping when searching for obscure information because the user isn't bombarded with irrelevant links.

See also: Internet, Link, Portal, Web Page

W

Wage

The compensation given to an employee in exchange for work performed.

What is considered a living wage in the Midwest won't get you very far in New York City.

See also: Compensation, Employee, Period

Warranty

A guarantee about the performance of a product, or a promise to perform a specific act, such as repairing or replacing a defective or broken product.

The warranty on the watch was void because the girl had tried to replace the battery herself.

See also: Customer Satisfaction, Performance, Quality

Wealth Effect
The theory stating that when people are wealthy, they will spend more money. Implicit in this is the assumption that when people become less wealthy, through everything from job loss to rising interest rates, they will spend less.

The low sales projections hadn't included the wealth effect caused by the federal government continuing to lower interest rates.

See also: Economics, Inflation, Leading Indicators

Wear and Tear
Slow physical decay of a product from use and age.

Even though the car was only a few years old, it was beginning to show the wear and tear caused by transporting three children regularly.

See also: Product, Productivity, Quality

Web Page
An online document or site.

The artist's Web page showed images of her work and gave a price list for each piece.

See also: Browser, Internet, Server, World Wide Web (WWW)

Webcast
Broadcasting over the Internet.

The professor aired a Webcast of her lectures for the online courses she taught.

See also: Communication, Internet, Multimedia

Webinar
A Web-based seminar; a presentation, lecture, workshop, or seminar that is transmitted over the Internet.

Everyone who used the autism chat room frequently was excited about the upcoming Webinar on the topic.

See also: Internet, Workshops, World Wide Web (WWW)

Webmaster
A businessperson who makes a living designing, developing, marketing, or maintaining Web sites.

As the webmaster for the site, it was Jessica's job to keep it updated and running smoothly.

See also: Advertising, Content, Coordinator, Internet, Marketing, Web Page

Wholesale Sales Method

The practice of selling to distributors, who in turn sell to full-service or self-service retail outlets, usually at prices that are significantly discounted over retail prices.

The wine-and-spirits industry employs middlemen to both distribute product and collect taxes for the state and federal government using the wholesale sales method.

See also: Distribution, Retailer, Sales

Wholesaling

All activities involved in selling goods or services to those who are buying for the purpose of resale or business use.

The merchant wholesaler performed all wholesaling functions with the exception of storage and handling.

See also: Distribution, Sales, Wholesale Sales Method

Wi-Fi

A wireless local area network used to connect to the Internet. Wi-Fi, a registered trademark, is short for wireless fidelity.

The baristas' tips increased when the coffee shop added Wi-Fi access because people would come and drink coffee all day while they worked from their laptops.

See also: Connectivity, Internet, Local Area Network (LAN), Network, Wireless

Wide Area Network (WAN)

A data communications network that covers a relatively broad geographic area and often uses transmission facilities provided by common carriers, such as telephone companies.

His job was to set up a wide area network that all employees could access.

See also: Data Communication, Extranet, Internet, Intranet, Local Area Network (LAN), Network

Windfall

An unexpected profit from a business or other source; implies a large profit without much, if any, work for it.

She felt guilty when she received her quarterly check and realized the high gas prices had turned into a windfall for her.

See also: Growth, Profit, Uncertainty, Windfall Tax

Windfall Tax

A tax levied by governments against certain industries when economic conditions allow those industries to experience above-average profits.

The state made sure all proceeds from the windfall tax went to improving the schools in the inner cities.

See also: Profit, Taxes, Windfall

Window of Opportunity

The time period during which a business, team, or project has a chance to make something happen.

The realtor knew he had a brief window of opportunity to sell the house before other realtors realized the property was on the market.

See also: Opportunities, Period, Project

Windows

The operating system created and trademarked by Microsoft that gives the user an easy-to-use point-and-click interface with icons on the desktop.

Windows is run by the vast majority of PC users.

See also: Computers, Icon, Interface

Withholding

The part of an employee's wages that are retained by the employer for contribution to taxes, health benefits, union dues, and other items.

The withholdings from his paycheck decreased his take-home pay dramatically.

See also: Benefits, Employee, Taxes

Work Breakdown Structure (WBS)

A list of all the tasks to be done for a project; deliverable-oriented hierarchy that depicts the work involved in an entire project.

A WBS explaining everyone's role in the project was delivered to the entire team.

See also: Hierarchy, Project Management, Task

Work Order

A request for a task or activity from one organization to another, usually within the same company.

The administrative assistant put in a work order for the IT department to fix three of the team's computers.

See also: Organization, Task

W

Worker's Compensation Insurance

Mandated insurance payments made by employers to cover their employees' work-related injuries and diseases; also known as "workman's comp."

The baggage handler has collected worker's compensation insurance ever since he threw out his back at work.

See also: Employee, Insurance

Working Capital

Cash available to an enterprise for day-to-day operations; the difference between current assets and current liabilities; the amount of funds available to pay short-term expenses.

The firm was widely invested, keeping only a minimum of working capital liquid and on hand.

See also: Cash, Current Assets, Current Liabilities, Operations

Workshops

An intensive course that provides opportunity for participants to hold a focused discussion in which they bring a common level of knowledge or skill to bear on a subject toward some practical end, such as developing a work in progress, solving problems, or developing new professional skills.

The training company offered workshops on everything from leadership to advanced computer skills.

See also: Group Process, Meeting, Teams

Workstation

A desktop computer where a knowledge worker performs daily tasks.

Most writers consider their workstations to be off limits to anyone but themselves.

See also: Computer, Desk Top, Network, Organized

World Wide Web (WWW)

The network that provides Internet users access to information online. The branch of the Internet that functions according to a constantly evolving set of protocols that allow servers and computer programmers across the world to share information in a digital format as a vast collection of information in hypertext and hypermedia format on home pages.

The World Wide Web has connected people and nations to an extent not even imagined prior to its existence.

See also: Hypertext, Link, Network

Write Off

To reassign a payment as an expense rather than a depreciable asset.

The accountant could not find an ethical way to consider the expense a write-off.

See also: Asset, Depreciation, Payments

Y

Year-to-Date (YTD)

The amount an account has accumulated since the first of the current year.

The profits year-to-date were far better than the store owners had expected.

See also: Accounting, Accounts, Period

Yield

The rate of return on an investment.

Although the 3.5 percent yield wasn't very good, he knew it was better than simply leaving the money in a savings account.

See also: Interest, Investment, Return on Investment (ROI)

Yield Curve

The difference between short-term and long-term interest rates.

The yield curve was good enough that she moved her savings from a short-term CD into a long-term money market.

See also: Economics, Interest Rates

Z

Zero-Based Budgeting

A budgeting strategy in which all costs, expenses, and investments are justified in each planning cycle.

The small manufacturing business instituted a zero-based budgeting system and improved their profits by 15 percent.

See also: Budget, Business Plan, Strategy

APPENDIX A

Acronym Appendix

Every industry has a language all its own and, as the demand for this book proves, business is no different. But even within the language of business, there is another language: one of acronyms. The assumption tends to be that if you are in on the conversation, you are in on the lingo. As most of us realize, however, that is not always the case. Therefore, consider this your cheat sheet. Here is a list of the acronyms found in this book and what they actually stand for. Now you can assure your COO that the RFP regarding the R&D for AI went out and the company can expect to start getting bids within the month—and know what you're talking about.

AI = Artificial Intelligence

APR = Annual Percentage Rate

ASP = Application Service Provider

ASP = Average Selling Price

BCG Box = Boston Consulting Group Box

B-to-B or B2B = Business-to-Business

B-to-C or B2C = Business-to-Consumer

BHAGs = Big, Hairy, Audacious Goals

CapEx = Capital Expenses

CEO = Chief Executive Officer

CFO = Chief Financial Officer

COB = Chairman of the Board

COD = Cash on Delivery

COGS = Cost of Goods Sold

COO = Chief Operating Officer

CPA = Certified Public Accountant

CPM = Critical Path Method

CRM = Customer Relationship Management

CSFs = Critical Success Factors

DBA = Doing Business As

DSS = Decision Support Systems

EBITDA = Earnings Before Interest, Taxes, Depreciation, and Amortization

ERP = Enterprise Resource Planning

EPS = Earnings Per Share

FIFO = First In First Out

G&A Expenses = General and Administrative Expenses

GAAP = Generally Accepted Accounting Principles

IP = Internet Protocol

IPO = Initial Public Offering

IRR = Internal Rate of Return

IT = Information Technology

JIT = Just-in-Time

LAN = Local Area Network

LBO = Leveraged Buyout

LIFO = Last In First Out

LLC = Limited Liability Company

LLP = Limited Liability Partnership

LOI = Letter of Intent

M&A = Mergers and Acquisitions

MBWA = Management by Walking Around

MIS = Management Information Systems

NDA = Nondisclosure Agreement

NPV = Net Present Value

NYSE = New York Stock Exchange

PDA = Personal Digital Assistant

P/E = Price/Earnings

PERT = Program Evaluation and Review Techniques

PEST = Political, Economic, Social and Technological

P&L = Profit and Loss

PLM = Product Life Cycle Management

PO = Purchase Order

POP = Point of Purchase

POS = Point of Sale

PPM = Private Placement Memorandum

RFP = Request for Proposal

ROA = Return on Assets

ROE = Return on Equity

ROI = Return on Investment

SAM = Served Available Market

SBU = Strategic Business Unit

SEC = Securities Exchange Commission

SMART = Specific, Measurable, Achievable, Relevant, and Time Bound

SOW = Statement of Work

SSFs = Strategic Success Factors

SWOT = Strengths, Weaknesses, Opportunities and Threats

TAM = Total Available Market

TMV = Time Value of Money

TQM = Total Quality Management

URL = Uniform Resource Locator

VOIP = Voice Over IP

VPN = Virtual Private Network

WAN = Wide Area Network

WBS = Work Breakdown Structure

WWW = World Wide Web

YTD = Year-to-Date